Y0-DOM-060

A Little Bit of
EVERYTHING

for Sixth Grade

by Laurie Gilbert

Illustrator

Milton Hall

Cover Artist

Laura Zarrin

Publisher
Instructional Fair • TS Denison
Grand Rapids, Michigan 49544

ISBN: 1-56822-883-X
A Little Bit of Everything for Sixth Grade
Copyright © 1998 by Instructional Fair • TS Denison
2400 Turner Avenue NW
Grand Rapids, Michigan 49544

Table of Contents

Introduction

This book consists of **A Little Bit of Everything for Sixth Grade**. It has been designed for the school-teacher or home school parent who is looking for review pages and additional teaching pages to complement his or her curriculum. Each page has been created to offer review and reinforcement for the sixth grader in all of the disciplines including reading, writing, English, language, spelling, math, science, geography, and history. Used as classroom handouts or as homework assignments, these worksheets will help make the teacher's job a bit easier.

Name _____

People Scavenger Hunt

Find someone in your class to sign each of the following. Each person can sign only once per sheet. Example: A student can sign size 6 shoes on one and an unusual pet on another, but not both on the same paper. See how many signatures you can get during the time limit your teacher gives you.

1. _____ Wears size 6 shoes
2. _____ Has a birthday on a holiday
3. _____ Has two or more brothers
4. _____ Has traveled out of the United States
5. _____ Has an unusual pet
6. _____ Collects stamps or coins or sports cards
7. _____ Plays soccer
8. _____ Has a red bicycle
9. _____ Can do a headstand
10. _____ Has no cavities
11. _____ Just moved to a new house
12. _____ Visited a zoo or museum during the past month
13. _____ Has a relative who works at the school
14. _____ Doesn't like pizza
15. _____ Has taken a train trip
16. _____ Rides the bus to school
17. _____ Has never eaten an avocado
18. _____ Has read any of Laura I. Wilder's Little House books
19. _____ Plays a musical instrument
20. _____ Has a fruit tree in his/her yard
21. _____ Family has a pick-up truck
22. _____ Is wearing a watch with a cartoon character on it
23. _____ is a Chicago Bulls basketball fan
24. _____ Likes country western music
25. _____ Favorite color is lavender

What was the most interesting thing you learned about one of your classmates that you did not know before? _____

Name _____

An Honest Look at Homework

Every person is unique. Every person has different ways for remembering things. What works for one person might not work for another. For example, some people are more alert and can think better in the morning, others at night. On the other hand, there are some things which are good for everyone, such as getting the right nutrients in your body and getting exercise. To be a better student, it is good to be aware of your own learning styles and habits and what really helps you to learn and remember. Be honest with yourself as you answer the following questions. What really works is better for you, not what you like better. Being willing to change some unhealthy habits can make you a better student.

1. When is the best time for me to study and do homework?
   a. after school   b. after dinner   c. early morning   d. other____

2. I study best and accomplish more
   a. when I'm alone   b. when I'm with other people

3. Where is the best place for me to study?
   a. my room   b. kitchen   c. family room   d. library   e. other_____

4. I can concentrate better if I'm
   a. lying down   d. walking around
   b. sitting at a desk   e. other _____
   c. sitting in a comfortable chair

5. I can accomplish my task more efficiently
   a. if it is quiet   b. with music (what type?)_____

*Studies have shown that baroque music creates the ideal mental state for learning.
   c. with TV   d. other _____

6. I can work best if I take a short break
   a. after 15 minutes   c. after one hour
   b. after ½ hour   d. when I'm completely finished

7. Will I study better if I have a snack? _____ What kind?
   a. no snack   d. fruit
   b. candy   e. cheese & crackers
   c. ice cream   f. other____

8. How will I reward myself for completing my assignments?
   a. take a break b. play a sport or game c. listen to music d. call a friend e. other _____

Now, make a plan for yourself based on your answers. Carefully follow your plan until it becomes natural.

Shoot to Win!

Someone once said that if we aim for nothing, we will hit it every time. How does that statement relate to having goals in your life? _____

Why do you think it is important to have goals? _____

What are some goals you want to accomplish this year?

    Social: What do I want to improve in my relationships with other people?

    Academic: What do I want to accomplish in school this year?

    Personal: Are there personal habits I can develop to help me be a better person?

    Physical: What can I do to keep my body healthy and physically fit?

Write your goals for each of these areas in the corresponding football below. On the lines, write what you can do to accomplish each of these goals.

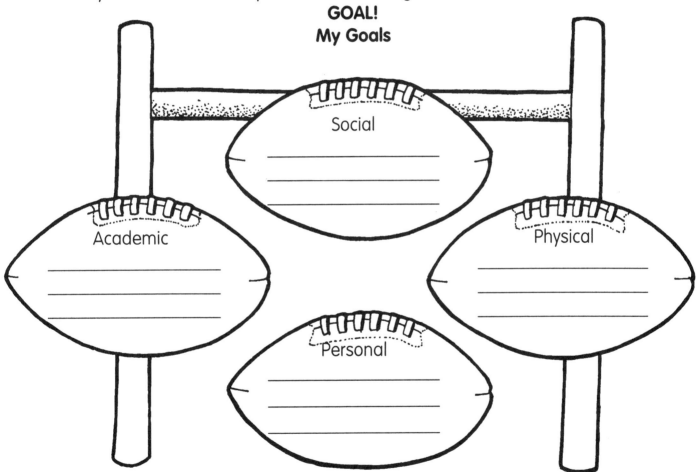

GOAL!
My Goals

Social

Academic

Physical

Personal

Keep this page in a place where you will look at it often to remind yourself of your goals and what you need to do to accomplish them.

One Step at a Time

Besides having long-range goals, it is good to have short-range goals—things you want to accomplish this week. These goals might be more specific than the long-range goals. Examples: I will practice piano for 20 minutes each day, or I will be at school on time every day this week, or I will score 100% on my spelling test this week. Challenge yourself when you set your goals, but be realistic, too. To help accomplish each of these goals, think of things you can do to make certain you succeed. Examples: I will practice piano right after school before I go out to play. I will wake up at 7:00 so I can be on time to school. I will write my spelling words three times and ask someone to help me study the evening before the test. Color the footprint each time you practice until your goal for the week is reached.

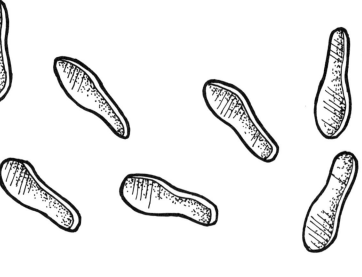

GOALS FOR THIS WEEK:

1. _____

2. _____

3. _____

WHAT I CAN DO TO SUCCEED:

_____
_____
_____
_____
_____

What can you do to reward yourself for the goals that you accomplish?

_____

Weekly Organizer

Name _____

week of _____

Use this form to plan your week. Fill in places you need to be, things you need to do, etc.

	Monday	Tuesday	Wednesday	Thursday	Friday	Saturday	Sunday
1st period							
2nd period							
3rd period							
4th period							
5th period							
6th period							
7th period							
8th period							
after school							
after dinner							
other things to schedule							

Name _____

Homework Record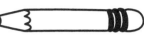

Use the first column to write your assignment, the second to check when you turn it in, and the third to record your grade.

Math	✓	%	English	✓	%
Science			Social Studies		
Reading			Spelling		
Health			Other		

Name _____

What Are Decimals Doing in the Library?

Nonfiction books in libraries are divided into different categories according to the main idea of each book. A man named John Dewey developed a numerical system for labeling the books, so it is called the Dewey Decimal System. Each book is assigned a number between 0 (000) and 999. This number is written or taped on the spine of the book along with the first three letters of the author's last name. This is referred to as the call number. The chart below will show what topic each set of 100 numbers represents.

000-099: General; encyclopedias, dictionaries, reference books
100-199: Philosophy
200-299: Religion (Bible, mythology, all religions)
300-399: Social Science (economics, political science, education)
400-499: Language (English as well as foreign languages)
500-599: Pure Sciences (including mathematics, biology, chemistry, physics)
600-699: Technology (applied science)
700-799: The Arts (including art, music, and sports and recreation)
800-899: Literature
900-999: History and geography (including biographies)

Once you learn this system, you can go to any library and find books on the topic you need by looking for the correct number. For example, if you wanted a book about Ancient Egypt, you would look in the 900 section for history books.

In which section would you look to find the following books?

1. You are learning to speak Spanish and you want a book to help you. _____
2. You are studying about Greece and want to read some Greek mythology. _____
3. You want to find a book on soccer to improve your skills. _____
4. Your teacher has just assigned a report on one of the countries of Africa. _____
5. You want to go stargazing so you need a book to explain the constellations and where to find them. _____
6. You are getting a new four-wheeler ATV. You want to understand about the engine and how it works. _____
7. You want to read about Abraham Lincoln. _____
8. You want a book to teach you how to draw horses. _____
9. You need a book to help you identify leaves in your neighborhood. _____
10. You are going to see a Shakespearean play and you want to read it first. _____

Name _____

Library Scavenger Hunt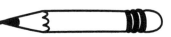

The clues below will help you to complete the scavenger hunt.
1. Fiction books are shelved in alphabetical order according to the author's last name. The first three letters of the author's last name are printed on the spine of the book along with an "F" for fiction.
2. Many libraries separate fiction books into three groups—adult fiction, young adult fiction, and children's or easy fiction.
3. Nonfiction books are shelved according to the Dewey Decimal system.
4. Magazines in libraries are called periodicals.
5. You can use the computer or card catalog to find books. All books are listed in three ways: 1) the title of the book; 2) the author; 3) the subject—what the book is about.
6. The number and letters found on the book's spine and on the corner of the card or on the computer screen are call numbers. They help identify the book.
7. If you cannot find what you are looking for, ask the librarian for help.

Locate and write the answers to each of the following.
1. The title of a young adult fiction book by Elizabeth George Speare.

    _____

2. Two periodicals in the library._____

    _____

3. The title, author, and call number of a book about rockets.

    _____

4. Who is the author of the children's fiction book **The Girl Who Loved Wild Horses**?

    _____

5. In the call number 351 Spr, what does 351 tell you?_____ Spr? _____

6. List three books (title, author) this library has about natural disasters. _____

    _____

7. Find an author who has written at least three fiction books. _____
    Titles of books:_____

8. In which periodical would you be likely to find an article about endangered species?

    _____

9. In which section of the 700s would you find books about music? _____
    What is the title of one book about music? _____

10. Ask your librarian to recommend a good book for you to read. What is the title, author, and call number? _____

Reference Extravaganza

To complete this activity, you will use the reference books in your library. These include encyclopedias, dictionaries, atlases, and almanacs. Write your answers on a separate sheet of paper.

1. Use an encyclopedia to find a flag for a country in Africa. Draw the flag.

2. Use an encyclopedia to look up a state in the United States. List its state tree, flower, bird, animal, and draw or describe its flag.

3. Use an almanac to find three countries with a population of less than 100,000.

4. Use an atlas. You are visiting Paris, France. List six countries you could visit without crossing a body of water.

5. Use an atlas to find five countries through which the equator passes.

6. Use an almanac to find out which country won the most gold medals in the 1996 Summer Olympics and the 1994 Winter Olympics.

7. Look up **plethora** in the dictionary. What part of speech is it? What does it mean?

8. Use an encyclopedia to look up Vincent Van Gogh or Pablo Picasso. When was he born? When did he die? Where did he live? What is the title of one of his art works?

9. Use an atlas. If you started at the tip of Florida and traveled east by boat around the world to California, through which bodies of water would you pass? List them in order.

10. Use an almanac to find out three things invented in the first half of the twentieth century (1900-1950). List what was invented, who invented it, and the date it was invented.

Name _____

Making an Outline ~~~~~~~~~~~~

You can use this outline to help organize information from a textbook, class notes, or for a research paper or report. The Roman Numerals (I, II, III) are the main ideas. The capital letters are important points for each main idea. The Arabic numerals are the supporting details for each main point. Sometimes each topic is further divided into smaller details (a, b).

Example: Title: Ancient China
  I. Shang Dynasty
      A. Geography
      B. Religion
  II. Qin Dynasty
      A. Government
      B. Building Projects
          1. Great Wall of China
          2. Emperor's Tomb

Title: _____

I.
  A.
      1.
      2.
  B.
      1.
      2.
  C.
      1.
      2.

II.
  A.
      1.
      2.
  B.
      1.
      2.
  C.
      1.
      2.

III.
  A.
  B.

IF8679 A Little Bit of Everything

Webbing

Name _____

Webbing is another way to organize information. The main topic is written in the center of the page. Pictures and key words or phrases are used for all the supporting details. Use this form for organizing information from a text book or class notes.

Example:

Name _____

To Do or Not to Do, That Is the Question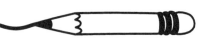

Every day we all have to make many decisions. Learning how to make good decisions is a skill that will be useful for the rest of your life. There are different kinds of decisions you will have to make. Sometimes you have an opportunity to do something and you just have to decide yes or no, should I or shouldn't I? A good way to help you think through the issue is to make a list of pros (the benefits or good things about doing it) and the cons (the drawbacks or negative consequences of doing it). Then you can look at both lists and see which side outweighs the other. Sometimes it helps to write down your lists. At other times you have to make a quick decision and do not have time to write down possibilities. Here's an example: Your best friend decides to try smoking and wants you to try it with him. What should you do?

Pros	Cons
-I'll look cool and grown up	-It's illegal at my age
-My friend will not get mad	-I could get addicted
	-It will cost a lot of money if it becomes a habit
	-It is very unhealthy—can cause lung cancer
	-It can be harmful to other people around me
	-My parents would be mad if they found out
	-It would harm my athletic endurance

1. Which side outweighs the other? _____

2. Why is that a better decision? _____

_____

3. Now you try. What is a decision you have to make? _____
    Pros   Cons

4. Which side outweighs the other? _____

5. Why is that a better decision? _____

Name _____

Too Many Choices, Too Little Time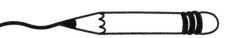

Some decisions we have to make involve many options. Some examples are choosing which book to read for a book report, what to buy with your $25.00 birthday check, or which after-school activities to join. Rather than making a pros and cons list for each option, you can use a chart to help make that decision. On one side of the chart, write all the options or choices you have. On the top write the criteria (what you base your decision on) you will use to rate each option. Example: Which book to read. Options: **Hatchet, Egypt Game, Boys Start the War**. Criteria: Which is more interesting to me? Which will I have time to read? Which will be easier to write a report about?

Now assign a number value. 5 is highest, and 1 is lowest.
Example: interesting topic—I like mysteries so
   Egypt Game is most interesting. I'll give it a 5.
   Survival stories are good. I'll give **Hatchet** a 4.
   The other book is about kids in a neighborhood–3.
Do the same with the other criteria.
Add the points in each row.
Which came out ahead?
Why is that a good decision?

	More Interesting?	Will I Have Time?	Better for a report	Total
Hatchet	4	4	3	11
Egypt Game	5	4	4	13
Boys Start the War	3	5	3	11

Here is a blank chart for you to use.
Decision:

Options   Criteria

Total

Which is the best decision? _____

Why? _____

Name _____

Memory Techniques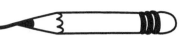

A big part of being a good student is having the ability to memorize. Here are some tricks to help you memorize things better.

1. Acronym: Take the first letters of the list of things you have to remember and make a word. Example: The Great Lakes—Huron, Ontario, Michigan, Erie, Superior—can make the word HOMES. What word could you use to remember the names of the three states on the west coast of the United States, Washington, Oregon, and California?_____

2. Some lists do not have first letters that will easily turn themselves into a word, so you could use an acrostic. Again, take the first letters of each word on the list and turn them into a funny saying to help you remember. Example: To memorize the names of the nine planets in the order from the closest to the sun and outward: My Very Educated Mother Just Showed Us Nine Planets (Mercury, Venus, Earth, Mars, Jupiter, Saturn, Uranus, Neptune, Pluto). What could you say to remember the categories for classifying organisms: Kingdom, phylum, class, order, family, genus, species?_____

_____

3. Another way to remember things is to put the information into a rhyme or song. For example: To remember when Columbus made his voyage to the new world, sing to the tune of "Mary Had a Little Lamb."
"Columbus sailed the ocean blue, ocean blue, ocean blue, Columbus sailed the ocean blue in fourteen hundred ninety-two." Think up a rhyme or song to remember that Johannes Gutenberg invented the printing press in 1448.

4. Pictures in your mind (or on paper) are easier to remember than words. Here are four clues to help make your pictures memorable. Make your picture silly or unusual, picture things bigger or more numerous than usual, or involve action. Example: Your mom sends you to the store to buy milk, eggs, and bananas. Picture a gallon of milk with a face and arms. He is juggling eggs and has a big banana in his mouth. What could you picture to help you remember the number of servings of each group on the food pyramid? _____

5. For new vocabulary words, you can think of something familiar that sounds similar. Example: **Pince nez**—glasses that sit on your nose, no ear pieces. Sounds like "pinch nose." How could you remember that **diversity** means differences or variety?_____

More Memory Techniques

Often we have to memorize lists of things in a particular order. We can use a system of peg words to help us remember them. Here is how one system works. For each number 1-10, think of a word picture that rhymes with the number. Example: 1-sun, 2-shoe, 3-tree, 4-door, 5-hive, 6-sticks, 7-heaven, 8-gate, 9-line, 10-pen. Now, in order to remember your list, you can connect each item with the peg word picture. The first would be pictured under the sun, the second with a shoe, the third with a tree, etc.

1. How could you use this system to remember a friend's phone number? Draw or explain your picture here.

2. You can use peg words to remember dates. Example: You have to remember that a friend's birthday is September (9) 21. Devise a system for remembering 9/21.

   Ask a friend his or her birthdate and then come up with a peg word picture to help you remember it.

3. You can also use phrases to help you remember things. To remember the order of the nine planets (except from 1980 to 2000), remember **M**y **V**ery **E**ager **M**other **J**ust **S**ewed **U**ncle **N**ed's **P**ants. Try to think of some other memory phrases. Do you know the man's name that should help you remember the color spectrum? _____

_____

If you would like to learn more about memory techniques, you can check a book out of the library on mnemonics (pronounced nee-MON-icks).

Name _____

Sarah Sees Seven Seashells

For each sentence, write the correct verb tense of the word given.

swim   1. Joel has _____ many times across the lake.

go   2. Victor _____ hunting last September.

wear   3. Don could have _____ the elf suit.

eat   4. Beth _____ less than her older sister.

choose   5. Chanda was _____ rhubarb queen of Polk County.

break   6. Who _____ the church window?

shrink   7. Lance was embarrassed to see how his swimsuit had _____.

blow   8. Hannah _____ out the candles on her cake.

fall   9. The tree has _____ on Abe's log cabin.

bring   10. The old woman _____ a candy cane to Hansel.

come   11. Who _____ in and forgot to wipe his feet?

sink   12. In dread, Lonnie _____ in her seat.

know   13. Rui should have _____ you were a vegetarian!

drink   14. David will _____ a glass of warm, sour milk.

run   15. The gingerbread man _____ into the barn.

ride   16. Has Christina _____ on a motorcycle before?

begin   17. The snow has _____ to come down hard.

freeze   18. Wanda _____ her toes when she chose sledding.

do   19. Marga has _____ her chores faithfully.

see   20. Sarah _____ seven seashells last Saturday.

Name _____

Mackinac Island

Sit, Set; Lie, Lay; Rise, Raise

Review the three sets of troublesome verbs listed above. As you read the paragraphs below, underline any of these verbs which have been used incorrectly. Some are used correctly. Rewrite the paragraphs, showing your corrections.

Mackinac Island

Mackinac Island is a three-mile-long and two-mile-wide island that sets in the Straits of Mackinac, the water that separates Michigan's Upper and Lower peninsulas. Lake Huron lays to the east of the island. French explorers sat foot on Mackinac Island first in the 1600s. It was an ancient Indian burial ground called Mishilimackinas by the Chippewas, meaning "great turtle" or "great spirit." The British later raised a fort there. After the United States lay claim to the island, John Jacob Aster sat up a fur company.

Today Mackinac Island is a popular summer resort. Jet boats whisk tourists from Mackinaw City and St. Ignace to Mackinac Island. When you sit foot on the island dock, you may feel as though you are in the eighteenth or nineteenth century. First of all, you will see horses and wagons going up and down the streets. There are no cars. Motor vehicles were banned in the late 1800s, so the only transportation is horse and wagon or bicycle.

As you raise early the next morning after your arrival, you may decide to tour the island. The first thing you see is someone raising the flag. Shops are beginning to open. Your favorite may be the fudge shop, where 30-pound slabs of fudge are setting on the counter to tempt you. Everything from antiques to T-shirts is available. As you roam the island, you cannot miss the century-old Grand Hotel, which sets on a hill above the village. It is a showplace with its 700-foot-long porch, yellow awnings, and American flags rippling in the breeze. White rocking chairs line the porch along with potted red geraniums. If you would like to set on this porch and watch the sun raise or set, just pay about $250 per night and you may.

Name _____

Pick a Pronoun

Circle the correct pronoun.

1. The last two guests were Tabitha and (he, him).
2. Could it be (she, her) who broke the chair?
3. The president gave Nancy and (he, him) ten dollars.
4. You and (I, me) have been chosen team captains.
5. Could you and (they, them) talk more quietly?
6. Mr. Smith showed my friend and (I, me) to our classes.
7. Our doctor told (we, us) boys that smoking was dangerous.
8. The telephone was ringing for you and (I, me).
9. (We, Us) musicians played the Bach piece grandly.
10. The artist taught (she, her) how to mold the clay.

Singular		Plural	
subject	**object**	**subject**	**object**
1. I	me	4. we	us
2. you	you	5. you	you
3. he, she, it	him, her, it	6. they	them

Fill in the blank with the appropriate pronoun from the box above.

1. Last Friday, Ted and _____ (1) went out for pizza.
2. _____ (4) humans certainly must recycle more often.
3. Could you have _____ (3) sign his autograph?
4. Mr. Thiele and _____ (3) showed us their cars.
5. Suddenly the ball sailed over _____ (6) into the bleachers.
6. Richard and _____ (6) never climbed the tower.
7. Please give _____ (1) a pony back ride!
8. When Katie came, _____ (4) asked _____ (3) to show _____ (4) the medals.
9. Would _____ (5) please complete this page for _____ (1)?

Name _____

Little Lottie Litchfield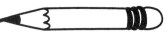

Write the comparative and superlative forms of each of these adjectives.

	comparative	superlative
1. large	_____	_____
2. cheerful	_____	_____
3. good	_____	_____
4. swift	_____	_____
5. frequent	_____	_____
6. bad	_____	_____
7. fancy	_____	_____
8. healthy	_____	_____
9. current	_____	_____
10. pleasant	_____	_____

Write the correct form of each word below.

1. sad I was _____ than you when we lost the game.

2. heavy The spotted pig was the _____ of the farm animals.

3. difficult Your job is _____ than his.

4. amazing Your pitching victory today is even _____.

5. careful Of all the kindergarteners, Allison is the _____.

6. cute I think the puppy looks _____ to you than it does to me.

7. funny Bernardo is the _____ boy on our block.

8. intelligent Randy's rabbit is _____ than a rooster.

9. short Rumpelstiltskin's house is the _____ on the block.

10. daring Little Lottie Litchfield was _____ than we expected.

Name _____

When, Where, and How?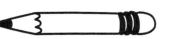

Many adverbs answer the questions **when**, **where**, or **how**. Underline the adverbs in the sentences below. If an adverb answers "when," write 1. If "where," write 2. If "how," write 3. For sentences with more than one adverb, write the numbers in the order that the adverbs appear.

1. Slick Steve streaked hurriedly into the classroom. _____

2. "I hate it here!" he cried anxiously. _____ _____

3. Fearfully the fledgling scholar tried to recall his studies. _____

4. "Yesterday I knew this junk well," he murmured. _____ _____

5. He now knew the meaning of the word terror. _____

6. Steve sat down abruptly at his desk. _____ _____

7. Then a brilliantly sparkling fairy sat down beside him. _____ _____ _____

8. What troubles you deeply?" asked the elfin creature who had suddenly appeared there. _____ _____ _____

9. "Who are you?" inquired Stevey incredulously. "Will you soon disappear?" _____ _____

10. Then the sparkling fairy lightly rapped Stevey's knuckles with her wand and said she would grant one wish if he faithfully promised to become a better student. _____ _____ _____

Write a different adverb to modify each verb.

1. dance _____   8. learn _____

2. write _____   9. sleep _____

3. smile _____   10. chew _____

4. tickle _____   11. kick _____

5. dash _____   12. wave _____

6. imagine _____   13. whisper _____

7. wash _____   14. stare _____

Name _____

Across the Page

In the directions below, underline each preposition. Then trace the path through the picture.

1. Start on the sidewalk.
2. Go towards the house.
3. Go in the door.
4. Go up the stairs.
5. Go out the window.
6. Go down the tree.
7. Go under the swing.
8. Go between the trees.
9. Go over the fence.
10. Go around the pond.
11. Go across the bridge.
12. Go through the flower garden.
13. Go back to the house.

Use prepositions to write directions for another path. Have someone follow your directions and trace the path through the picture below.

1. _____
2. _____
3. _____
4. _____
5. _____
6. _____
7. _____
8. _____
9. _____
10. _____
11. _____
12. _____

The Conjunction Connection

Circle the conjunctions in the sentences below.

1. Jack rolled down the hill before Jill could stop him.
2. Until Miss Muffet came, the spider had no one to frighten.
3. The cat played the fiddle, and the dog jumped extremely high.
4. Little Red Riding Hood screeched when she saw her "grandma's" teeth.
5. The old man snored whether it rained or not.
6. When H. Dumpty had a great fall, we feasted on omelets for weeks.
7. The third pig made his house of bricks because he had studied lupine behavior.
8. Jack traded his cow for beans, but this did not please his mother.
9. While the blue-clothed boy slept, cows chewed the field corn.
10. There was a crooked man, although orthopedic surgery was available.

Combine the sentences below using conjunctions from this list:

after   as   if   since   so that   and

1. Hansel dropped bread crumbs. The birds ate all the crumbs.

   _____

2. We marveled at Mary's garden. She grew silverbells so well.

   _____

3. The small goat crossed the bridge. The medium-sized goat tried his luck.

   _____

4. Peter put his wife in a pumpkin shell. She had plenty to eat.

   _____

5. Three men floated in a tub. They sang a pleasant song.

   _____

6. Mary had a little lamb. It had a fluffy, white coat.

   _____

Name _____

Oh, Yeah!

Circle the interjections in the sentences below.

1. Ouch! That hurt my feelings!

2. We won the game? Yippee!

3. Oh, yuck! We're having sirloin steak again.

4. Goodness gracious! You sure have grown, Erin!

5. Hooray! We have school today!

6. Get out of that tree! Hey! You over there!

7. Ugh! The kitchen smells like rotten eggs!

8. You're going to New York? Hallelujah!

9. Hello! Is anybody there?

10. Good grief! The little red-hired girl is looking at me!

Be creative. Write a different interjection for each of these sentences.

1. _____! My toe got stuck in the drain!

2. _____! You're asking me to go to a movie with you?

3. _____! This porridge is just right!

4. _____! That race really tired me out!

5. _____! Where did I put that twenty-dollar bill?

6. _____! I can't believe you'd do such a thing!

7. _____! Who will lead our team now?

8. _____! The grease just stained my shirt!

9. _____! I've been named Mr. Universe!

10. _____! I never want to go there again!

Name _____

"Object"ively Speaking

Underline the direct object in each sentence.

1. King Kong destroyed my uncle's grocery.

2. Grandma Adams poured lemonade into our glasses.

3. Anna loved dogs and cows.

4. Brian's dad painted the living room yesterday.

5. The young goat loved oats more than rye.

6. I wrote a fantastic novel.

7. The silly rabbit gobbled the head of lettuce.

8. Penny bought a nickel for a quarter.

9. Felix, the gardener, spied three roses.

10. The French poodle from Denmark bit a German tourist in Turkey.

Underline the direct object and place the indirect object in parentheses.

1. Josey saved me the last doughnut on the plate.

2. Tanya told Teddy a tale of two turtles.

3. I gave myself a hundred dollars!

4. Harvey handed Horace a huge hamburger.

5. Patsy threw Sally the football.

6. Sarah sent her aunt a signed photograph of Barney the Dinosaur.

7. Bethany offered Valerie a bucket of soapy water.

8. Katie couldn't quite catch Kendra the crickets she craved for her critter collection.

9. The zookeeper fed his piranha bits of Butterfinger bars.

10. The advertisement offered Gullible Gary a trip to Cincinnati.

Name _____

Parts of Speech

In each column, list ten words or phrases. For an extra challenge, have each row start with the same letter or have a minimum number of letters.

	nouns	verbs	adjectives	adverbs	prepositional phrases
1.					
2.					
3.					
4.					
5.					
6.					
7.					
8.					
9.					
10.					

How many sentences can you create in ten minutes using one word or phrase from each column?

1. _____

2. _____

3. _____

4. _____

5. _____

6. _____

7. _____

8. _____

9. _____

10. _____

Name _____

The Wastebasket

All the quotation marks plus the commas, periods, question marks, and exclamation marks which are used before and after quotations are missing in this humorous story. Rewrite the story on another sheet of paper, adding necessary punctuation and paragraphing. You may want to add punctuation marks in pencil on the copy below before you recopy it.

The Wastebasket

Just the other day the teacher asked Tim Will you empty the wastebasket and then lead the class in the pledge to the flag Tim said Yes However when he went to empty the wastebasket, it ran away from him. He and the teacher went running down the hall, chasing the wastebasket. Oh, no Tim cried It's going into the principal's office The principal was holding an important meeting and was startled by the intrusion of Tim, his teacher, and the wastebasket. What is going on here the principal shouted Tim, why are you chasing the wastebasket and, Mrs. Jones, why are you out of your classroom? What is this ridiculous wastebasket doing in my office Tim felt awful and could not say a word. Mrs. Jones told him Go back to the classroom and begin the pledge to the flag. I'll be there shortly So Tim hurried back to the classroom and had all the students stand. He started to lead the pledge: I pledge allegiance to the flag.... When he began to say the pledge, the flag rolled up. When he stopped reciting the pledge, the flag unrolled. Of course, all the students started giggling. Tim could not understand what was going on and thought someone was playing a joke on him. Okay, what's going on here he asked Who's the wise guy He had already been in trouble once and did not want to get in trouble twice in the same day. Mrs. Jones had heard the laughter and raced back to the classroom to quiet the class. Quiet she yelled You are disturbing all the classes When she saw why the students were all laughing, she burst into laughter too. By this time the principal heard the laughter and stormed toward the uproar. As he neared the classroom door, he shouted If you do not stop laughing, you will all stay after school But no one could hear him because they were all laughing so hard; and when he saw what was happening, he started laughing along with the rest. Soon all the students in the school had crowded into or near the classroom, and everyone joined in the laughter.

Name _____

Add the Apostrophes

Place the apostrophes where they belong.

1. My mothers cat lost its play toy.

2. Didnt I see you at the three boys playhouse?

3. Shirley couldnt believe that Franks dog barked like that!

4. The red birds feathers ruffle when the winds blowing.

5. Are clocks always set ahead when its daylight-saving time?

6. "Youre supposed to obey the teachers rule!" snapped Betsys sister.

7. Whereve all the flowers gone?

8. My cousins house isnt anywhere near Port Royal Road.

9. Why wont you be Pattys valentine?

10. Oh, were going to Grandmas house on Sunday.

11. If wed known hed be there, we wouldve brought Berts bike.

12. The childs uncles name appeared on many newspapers headlines.

13. If Seths coming to Nates house, hed better get here soon.

14. The bulk of five sumo wrestlers weight rested on the hood of Matts Toyota.

Write the words below as contractions.

1. is not   _____

2. could not   _____

3. shall not   _____

4. let us   _____

5. he is   _____

6. we are   _____

7. here is   _____

8. will not   _____

9. has not   _____

10. she will   _____

Name _____

Hmm, What Do I Need?

Insert colons, semicolons, and commas where they are needed.

1. We will have breakfast at 715 A.M.

2. The boys caught the young calf they returned it to its pen.

3. When the large boisterous and fun-loving man joined us we laughed for hours.

4. We play trombone for our school band our director says we are very good.

5. Dear Sir or Madame

    Please send me your latest copy of **Boy's Life**.

6. The following students will serve on the panel Peter Jeremy Tara and Kim.

7. At 400 P.M. we stopped work at 600 P.M. our baseball game got underway.

8. Steve can you spell the following **souffle spaghetti sherbet** and **cappuccino**?

9. Let's give the dessert to Leah Dave she hasn't eaten since 830 this morning.

10. This is the list of purchases we made two sweaters candy canes a box of toothpicks four pens and a photo album.

11. Her face turned toward us her smile radiated its own light.

12. Joe hear the words I give to you and then go to the doctor.

13. The bus leaves at 210 P.M. and the train departs at 305 P.M.

14. The sky burst open the rain poured down like a waterfall.

15. To whom it may concern

    My house is neither a zoo a farm nor a kennel. Please tie up your dog and clean up behind your pet when you must take it out.

16. Sara loves the sea it gives her inspiration.

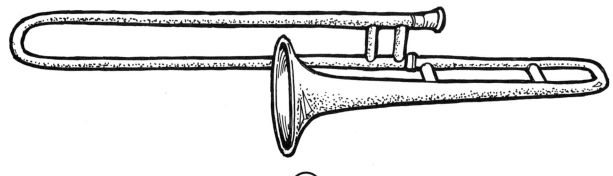

Name _____

What Is It?

Punctuate the end of each sentence. Then write whether the sentence is a statement, question, command, or exclamation.

1. What a great party we had   _____

2. What made it such a great event   _____

3. The food was pizza, and the music was perfect   _____

4. Please speak a little louder   _____

5. Can't you hear me   _____

6. Of course I can't, silly   _____

7. Well, the music was loud, but the sound was excellent   _____

8. I wish I could have been there   _____

9. Are you going to Rosie's next week   _____

10. Man, I wouldn't miss it for the world   _____

11. Call me later this week   _____

12. Do you need to get off the phone already   _____

13. Yeah, I've got work to do for my mom   _____

14. That's a real bummer, guy   _____

15. Hey, watcha doing in an hour   _____

16. I'll be sitting here like a bump on a log   _____

17. Well, come on by, and we'll shoot some hoops   _____

18. Hey, sounds great   _____

19. Bring your air pump 'cuz my basketball is low on air   _____

20. I'll be over in a bit   _____

Name _____

A Troubling Tale

Edit the verbs in each sentence so that the story is written correctly in past tense.

1. The little, red-cloaked child like to visit her adoring grandma.

2. Her kind and thoughtful mama pack a delicious lunch, which she then place in a wicker basket.

3. Off skip the hooded child along the flowered pathway.

4. Unknown to the lass, a wicked wolf were waiting for her.

5. "Hello!" cry the wolf in a friendly voice. "What is you doing?"

6. "Oh, I is on my way to my grandma's. She are feeling sickly," reply the child.

7. "Why, then I must pays her a visit," mew the wolf in a courteous manner.

8. So off he scamper down a secret side path while the wee child dawdle on the pathway picking posies.

9. Arriving at the grandma's quaint cottage, the sinister beast thrusts the old woman into the closet, disguise himself as the grandma, and plop into her four-poster bed.

10. About 20 minutes later, the red-hooded juvenile knock on the cottage door saying, "Hi, Gram! It are me, Rosie!"

11. In a high-pitched but very poorly rendered "grandma" voice, the sharp-toothed canine squeak, "Comes in, dearie, and visited with your granny."

12. Stomping briskly through the entryway, Rosie step into her granny's bedroom and stop suddenly at the foot of the bed.

Now finish the story on another sheet of paper. Include past tense forms of these verbs: shout, sneer, race, climb, twitch, and blink.

Name _____

The Electric Impact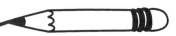

Copy the following paragraphs on a separate sheet of paper and insert all needed capitals and punctuation necessary to correct fragments and run-on sentences.

The Electric Impact

There are some advantages of having an electric car general Motors' Impact is a good example it has power, goes from a standstill to 60 mph instantly, and handles well on the road the dashboard in the Impact gives a wealth of information in addition to telling the speed, it shows how far you can go before recharging if you happen to forget that the car is plugged into an electric socket, there is a warning light also the words "check messages" flash when the warning lights go on somewhere else the dashboard will also tell the driver of any motor or battery problems, if there is a low tire, or if the road is slick.

Doesn't all this sound wonderful well, it is however, one big problem is that if you run out of juice, you cannot stop at someone's house and plug the car into an outlet for a short time and then go on your way it takes 3 to 12 hours to charge the battery there's the possibility that you may forget to plug in the car overnight in that case you may have to find another way to get to work or to school the next morning.

37

Name _____

What's the Point?

Underline the topic sentence in each paragraph below.

1. Stephanie didn't know what to do. She had already read all of the books she owned. She started to bake a cake until she remembered they were out of flour. She clicked on the television in the playroom. Only boring cartoons were on. Grumpily, Stephanie clambered up into the porch hammock and fell asleep.

2. When I woke up this morning, I had a headache. I hopped out of bed and tripped on my brother's blocks. Then I discovered that Puffy, my cocker spaniel, had chewed up my slippers. This was the lousiest day of my life. After sprinkling sugar on my corn flakes, I learned that my brother had switched the sugar for salt.

3. Rachel raced across the park. She dashed north along Cherry Street and turned left on Fulton. She spun up her driveway, climbed the back steps two at a time, and tore open the screen door. Leaping over Lizzie, her kid sister, Rachel reached for the refrigerator door. She pulled out the pitcher of cold, freshly pressed apple cider and poured a cup. Sometimes you need a cold drink to keep you going.

4. Now this was the life! Ben and his dad set up their two-man tent together. While Dad got out the food for dinner, Ben gathered the wood for the fire. Before sunset, they had finished their meal and had time to walk to the lake to see the loons. Ben loved camping

5. What our school needs is a swimming pool. Swimming is one of the best means of exercise. If we had a pool, we could open our building to the community in the evening. Our students could take swimming and lifesaving classes. Our swim team could train here instead of across town. Please vote yes on this issue next week.

Walt Disney

As you read about Walt Disney, you should find a number of errors in spelling, capitalization, punctuation, and usage. After identifying the errors, copy the selection and correct all errors.

Walt Disney

Walt Disney once said like most people, I have fun just watching others have fun. Many of you have probably visited Disneyland an amusement park in Anaheim california or Disney World near orlando Florida. Im sure youre familar with characters like Mickey mouse and Donald duck but do you know much about the person responsable for these places and characters. Many years ago before you were even born Walt disney began creating carton film characters. Then he produced full-length cartoon movies and movies about wild animuls.

Walt Disney was born in Chicago Illinois in 1901. When he was a child his family moved from Chicago to missouri. He spent much of his boyhood on a farm near Marceline where he aquired a love for animals. He later studied art in Chicago at the age of 18 but in his early twenties he moved to Los Angeles Calivornia. Walt worked hard for a few years just making enough to pay his bills. Then Mickey Mouse saved him! Walts first short Micky Mouse film was a hit this lead to more cartoons with characters like Donald duck, Goofy, and Pluto and finaly to movies such as **Snow White and the Seven Dwarfs Bambi Cinderella**, and **Lady and the Tramp**.

Probably Walt Disneys greatest success came when he opened Disneyland an amusement park unlike any other park. At the time he was ridiculed by other amusement park owners. They told him you will never succeed with this idea this is just like all the other amusement parks Walt proved them wrong. He planned a similiar park Walt Disney World in Florida. It was completed in 1971 after his death in 1966. It continues to bee a very popular vacation spot for children and adults. Why was Walt Disney so successful. It was probably because of hard work practical knowledge, and foresight. Maybe theirs a lesson hear for all of us.

Editor's Checklist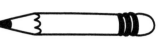

Use the checklist below when proofreading the final draft of any written material. It will help you to remember things you may have forgotten.

☐ Does each sentence begin with a capital letter and end with a period, question mark, or exclamation mark?

☐ Does each sentence have a subject and verb and a complete thought?

☐ Are there any fragments or run-on sentences?

☐ Are all words capitalized that should be?

☐ Are all words spelled correctly?

☐ Have you used any troublesome verbs? If so, have you used the correct forms?

☐ Does each subject agree with its verb?

☐ Does each pronoun agree with the word it refers to (antecedent)?

☐ Have you used apostrophes correctly—to show omission of letters or possession?

☐ Are the exact words of a speaker enclosed in quotation marks?

☐ Have all necessary commas and semicolons been correctly inserted?

☐ Have you checked the grammar and usage in your writing?

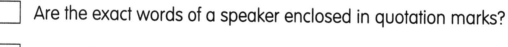

Name _____

Silence Is Golden

Supply the missing "silent" letters for the words below.

1. ans __ er
2. __ nat
3. sta__k
4. glis __ en
5. lim __
6. mi __ t
7. vale __
8. wi __ ch
9. __ onor
10. Siou __
11. wou __ d
12. bri __ ge
13. rei __ n
14. physiq __
15. whis __ le
16. ou __ t
17. __ reath
18. tom __
19. s __ ord
20. si __ n
21. __ ritten
22. pa __ ch
23. sil __ ouette
24. Chevrole __
25. thou __
26. bolo __ na
27. ___ sychic

28. r __ yme
29. We __ nesday
30. colo __ ne
31. le __ pard
32. Illinoi __
33. ca __ f
34. __ nit
35. __ our
36. buffe __
37. r __ ubarb
38. __ onest
39. fou __ t
40. __ salm
41. gourme __
42. campai __ n
43. Arkansa __
44. we __ ge
45. bere __
46. t __ o
47. shou __ d
48. cas __ le
49. r __ ombus
50. uniq __
51. le __ ge
52. __ terodactyl
53. wa __ ch
54. ___ nome

You're a Pro!

Name _____

To complete the magic square, write the number of a word from the list in the lettered square that corresponds to its definition. Two of the words will not be used.*

1. probe
2. produce
3. profane
4. promise
5. profound
6. progress
7. prohibit
8. project
9. prolong
10. promote
11. pronoun
12. pronounce
13. propel
14. proportion
15. propose
16. prosper
17. protein
18. provoke

A. create; grow vegetables
B. to stop
C. stir up; make angry
D. speak clearly; articulate
E. stick out; a plan
F. deep and intense
G. a replacement for a noun
H. suggest
I. move forward
J. an essential part of diet
K. growth; to improve
L. blasphemous
M. have good fortune
N. to raise to a higher level
O. agreement to do something
P. to lengthen

A	B	C	D
E	F	G	H
I	J	K	L
M	N	O	P

*Check your magic square by adding each row and then each column of numbers. If all the sums are the same, you have matched correctly.

Write the two words that were not included in the square.

1. _____ 2. _____

Write the six words that can be used either as nouns or as verbs.

1. _____ 4. _____
2. _____ 5. _____
3. _____ 6. _____

Let's Write! Write a letter to your teacher in which you propose a change for the classroom, a field trip, or a class project. Tell how your proposal would promote thinking and learning. Describe some of the things your proposal might prohibit. Be profuse in your use of words from the list.

Name _____

Classified Ads

Write each word in the proper category (noun, verb, or adjective). Be careful. Some words can be more than one part of speech. Write them under the appropriate categories.

adventure

advise

advantage

adopt

admire

adjective

address

admit

advance

adult

advent

admonish

adapt

adhere

adjust

adequate

advice

adorn

Noun

1. _____
2. _____
3. _____
4. _____
5. _____
6. _____
7. _____
8. _____

Verb

1. _____
2. _____
3. _____
4. _____
5. _____
6. _____
7. _____
8. _____
9. _____
10. _____
11. _____

Adjective

1. _____
2. _____
3. _____

Let's Write! Write a classified ad for a newspaper using at least five of the words from the list.

Example: **"Adults** wanted. Please **adopt** my pet mouse. Mice **adapt** easily to new surroundings. My mom **admonished** and **advised** me to give him up."

Arithmetician/Magician

Change each word from the list to a possessive noun by adding an 's. Use the clues to write the correct possessive noun on each blank.

arithmetician
beautician
clinician
diagnostician
dietician
electrician
magician
mathematician
mortician
musician
obstetrician
optician
Phoenician
physician
politician
statistician
technician
theoretician

1. _____ ancient alphabet
2. _____ funeral home
3. _____ diagnosis
4. _____ stethoscope
5. _____ shampoo
6. _____ eye chart
7. _____ formulas
8. _____ statistics
9. _____ numbers

10. _____ theory
11. _____ cello
12. _____ rabbit
13. _____ clinic
14. _____ wires
15. _____ patient
16. _____ speech
17. _____ menu
18. _____ machine

All of the words from the list except one identify occupations. Research that word and write a short description of your findings.

_____

_____

Make a list of your own words. _____

Make any of your own words that are nouns possessive by adding 's or s'. _____

_____

Let's Write!
Which of the occupations found in your spelling list most appeals to you? Which interests you the least? For each choice, write a paragraph detailing your reasons.

Name _____

Fractured Compounds

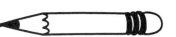

Each exercise below lists three compound words with the first part missing. Find the word in the Word Box that completes each word. Write it in the first blank.

Word Box			
air	lady	bed	pay
key	back	off	counter
arch	mill	bob	road
free	green	dead	egg
ring	rose	pull	

1. _____	___side	___bed	___block
2. _____	___bug	___love	___finger
3. _____	___mail	___line	___sick
4. _____	___bud	___wood	___bush
5. _____	___duke	___enemy	___angel
6. _____	___board	___stone	___note
7. _____	___sled	___cat	___white
8. _____	___back	___over	___out
9. _____	___man	___hand	___way
10. _____	___race	___stone	___stream
11. _____	___load	___off	___roll
12. _____	___house	___horn	___back
13. _____	___pane	___balance	___clockwise
14. _____	___stage	___shoot	___shore
15. _____	___lock	___beat	___line
16. _____	___plant	___head	___beater
17. _____	___leader	___worm	___master
18. _____	___space	___bone	___fire
19. _____	___spread	___time	___room

Challenge: Write three compound word problems of your own.

1. _____ _____ _____ _____

2. _____ _____ _____ _____

3. _____ _____ _____ _____

Name _____

Long Form

Complete the puzzle by writing the word for each abbreviation.

Across

2. chem.
5. oz.
8. Fri.
11. lb.
12. Am.
15. mpg
17. l.
18. conj.
19. W
20. prep.
21. P.M.

Down

1. yr.
3. min.
4. qt.
6. ex.
7. MT
9. lt.
10. n.
13. NW
14. 2nd
15. Mr.
16. Pres.

46

Name _____

What's It All About?

Read the sentences. Write the letter of the definition that best matches the word in bold.

Definitions		
a. searched	f. behind a vessel	k. nonsense
b. to waste time	g. select	l. gallows
c. a song	h. a small container	m. long-wooled sheep
d. a small child	i. of the eye	n. untamed
e. lively	j. gloomily	o. to praise

1. The prisoner trudged slowly to the **gibbet** contemplating his forthcoming death.

2. "Aye there, Captain. We've got some movement **astern.**"

3. The boy sat **morosely** waiting for his father whose car he had recently dented.

4. The princess held up a **cruse** of a magical lotion with which she could heal all injuries.

5. The **tyke** looked up at the college student and marveled at his height.

6. Sherry was acting as wild as a **feral** mustang.

7. Please **cull** the overripe peaches from the rest of the peck.

8. His excuse for being late was merely **hokum.**

9. The **chanson** we heard brought tears to our eyes.

10. The **ocular** scarring left him worried about his chances of obtaining a driver's license.

11. "I wish to **tout** 'Wheato-grahams' as the most wholesome of all fake food," proclaimed the actor.

12. For such an elderly person, Aunt Elvira certainly is **sprightly.**

13. The pirating mob **ransacked** our minivan.

14. "Now, Little Red Riding Hood, please don't **dilly-dally** on your way to Grandmama's house," reminded her mother.

15. The **merino** grazed in the pastureland, not knowing the wolf was but a stone's throw away.

47

Name _____

Opposing Views

Match each vocabulary word with the letter of its antonym.

Vocabulary Words

1._____ imperative
2._____ adhere
3._____ wit
4._____ solemn
5._____ save
6._____ pessimistic
7._____ gorgeous
8._____ zeal
9._____ endanger
10._____ guilt
11._____ true
12._____ remnant
13._____ law
14._____ increase
15._____ credible
16._____ distant
17._____ remember
18._____ remain
19._____ beginning
20._____ hasty
21._____ thin
22._____ opaque
23._____ youthful
24._____ unique

Antonyms

a. unfasten
b. fictional
c. depart
d. confident
e. pudgy
f. unattractive
g. unbelievable
h. chaos
i. methodical
j. stupidity
k. conclusion
l. whole
m. optional
n. forget
o. elderly
p. squander
q. protect
r. clear
s. diminish
t. hilarious
u. common
v. innocence
w. apathy
x. close

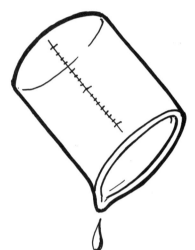

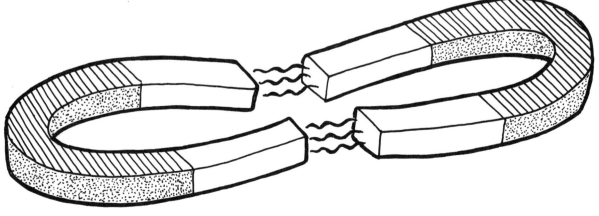

Name _____

A Perplexing Problem to Ponder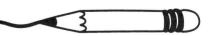

Alliteration is using words all, or almost all, starting with the same letter. See if you can write a sentence for each letter of the alphabet. Letter "A" is done for you.

A - An angry alligator ate an awkward aardvark on an afternoon in August.

B -

C -

D -

E -

F -

G -

H -

I -

J -

K -

L -

M -

N -

O -

P -

Q -

R -

S -

T -

U -

V -

W -

X -

Y -

Z -

Use these sentences to make an alphabet book. Write and illustrate each sentence on a separate page.

A Page for a Sage

Below are clues to pairs of rhyming words. Pairs of one-syllable words are ink-pinks.

1. a tube for draining the excess moisture from the breathing appendix on your face:

   _____

2. a tree branch for doing amazing acts: _____
3. a vehicle for transporting web-footed fowl: _____
4. a dwelling for a rodent: _____
5. phobia of Bambi and his family: _____
6. a distant celestial object: _____
7. a lizard that lives on apples and oranges: _____
8. a path for a hopping reptile: _____
9. a container for woolen foot coverings: _____
10. an escaped gander: _____

Pairs of two-syllable rhyming words are inky-pinkies.

1. a bright primary-colored wobbly dessert: _____
2. a dent in the chrome projection of the front of a car: _____
3. electrical outlet on a space vehicle: _____
4. an obstruction for a shelled reptile: _____
5. one who eats way too much meat from old sheep: _____
6. a soft cushion for resting your head stuffed with leaves from a weeping tree:

   _____

7. a particular window covering: _____
8. a cubicle for equipment of a particular type of sports team: _____
9. identification tag for a flat-topped piece of furniture: _____
10. a tall building made of roses and tulips: _____

Pairs of rhyming words with three or more syllables are inkity-pinkities.

1. protection of Native American lands: _____
2. a word processor for one who travels to work: _____

Make up some of your own and have your friends try to guess the answers.

_____

_____

_____

_____

Name _____

As Alike as Two Peas in a Pod

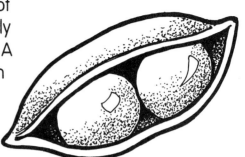

A simile is a comparison using the words **like** or **as** (not to be confused with, "Like, Dude, that was like, so totally awesome!"). Similes are used to create word pictures. A mother who is trying to hurry her slow-moving children along so they won't be late might say, "and you're off like a herd of turtles," as they go out the door.

Fill in the blanks with words to complete each simile.

as dry as _____   as cold as _____

as pretty as _____   as quiet as _____

as slow as _____   as smooth as _____

as big as _____   as green as _____

as mischievous as _____   as sly as _____

as busy as _____   as hard as _____

as colorful as _____   as quick as _____

as gentle as _____   as peaceful as _____

as easy as _____   as funny as _____

lined up like _____

blue like _____

falling down like _____

laughing like _____

eating like _____

running like _____

piling up like _____

climbing like _____

flying through the air like _____

shooting the basketball like _____

Sometimes a simile can be used to show contrast. Look at the following example. I knew my mother was upset because her voice sounded about as calm as a tornado. Can you think of other examples using a simile to show a contrast?

_____

_____

_____

Name _____

The Bare Bear Ate Eight Pairs of Pears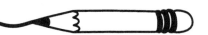

Homophones are words that sound alike, but are spelled differently and have different meanings. Write down all the pears (or is it pairs?) of homophones that you can think of in the next few minutes.

These are illustrations of homophones. Can you guess what they are? The first one is done for you.

bare   bear

_____   __   _____   _____   _____

Draw your own illustrations of other pairs of homophones on your list.

Name _____

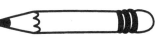

Rest in Peace

Some words in our language get overused. Just for fun, let's put some of these words to rest as if they were no longer part of our language and try using others instead. Each of the words in the tombstones has been eliminated. Make a list of synonyms, or other words you could use in its place. If you are stumped, use a thesaurus.

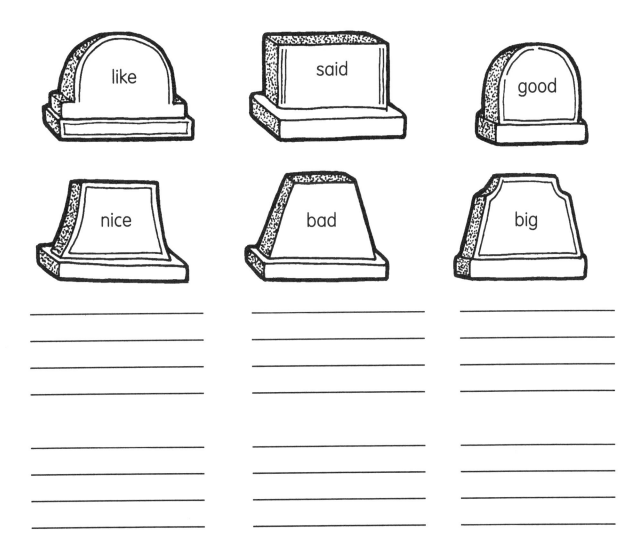

Challenge: Every time you are tempted to use one of the old, extinct words above, try using one of the new words instead.

Name _____

Sing Is to Song, as . . .

Complete each phrase.

1. glue is to sticking as pencil is to _____
2. son is to mother as daughter is to _____
3. country is to continent as city is to _____
4. 5 is to 15 as 4 is to _____
5. garage is to car as library is to _____
6. Victoria is to lake as Pacific is to _____
7. hot is to steam as cold is to _____
8. weak is to strong as good is to _____
9. hair is to human as _____ are to trout
10. 2 is to bicycle as 3 is to _____
11. clipper is to sail as _____ is to paddle
12. drama is to act as ballet is to _____
13. knock is to rap as _____ is to delay
14. adios is to Spanish as au revoir is to _____
15. pilot is to aircraft as nurse is to _____
16. Damascus is to Syria as Tokyo is to _____
17. moo is to herd as _____ is to flock
18. lion is to pride as wolf is to _____
19. racket is to tennis as club is to _____

IF8679 A Little Bit of Everything

Recipe Poem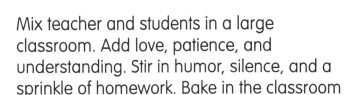

Developing Skills
Students will use cooking terms with other nouns, ordinarily not associated with cooking, to write a recipe poem.

Resources
Cookbooks and recipes

Prewriting
Organize cooperative learning groups of four to six students. Give each group a variety of cookbooks and recipes. Each group selects a recorder. Then, students browse through the cookbooks to find verbs that apply to cooking. The recorder keeps a list of such terms for the group on chart paper. Examples: bake, peel, mash, cook, mix, sprinkle, stir, chop, etc. Students also look for nouns that name measurements often used in cooking— cup, teaspoon, tablespoon, ounce, etc.

Writing
Explain that each student in the group will write a recipe for success at school. The student lists the ingredients and gives directions for success.

Example:

Success at School
Ingredients:
1 teacher
25 students
1 cup of love
2 cups of patience
½ cup of understanding
dash of humor
1 tablespoon of silence
sprinkle of homework
1 pint of cheerfulness

Mix teacher and students in a large classroom. Add love, patience, and understanding. Stir in humor, silence, and a sprinkle of homework. Bake in the classroom for one year. Spread cheerfulness on top and serve warm to everyone.

Responding
Each student shares his/her recipe for success with the group. Members of the group make suggestions for improving the recipe.

Revising/Editing
Each author may choose to revise his/her poem as suggested by the response group. Then, the student checks spelling.

Postwriting
Each student writes his/her recipe for school success on an 8½" x 11" sheet of paper and decorates it. Place all the recipes in a class book. Then, the author writes his/her recipe on a file card to keep.

Evaluating
The student made two copies of his/her poem in neat handwriting. The student participated in the cooperative learning group.

Extending Writing
Have students collect favorite recipes and write a class cookbook for Mother's Day.

Have students write recipes for a variety of topics: "Fun with My Family," "How to Make Friends," etc.

Haiku

Developing Skills
Students will learn the form of haiku poetry. They will learn syllabication.

Prewriting
Use this lesson as a culminating activity for a unit on water fowl or autumn. Explain that haiku is an ancient form of Japanese poetry that is most often about nature. The poems follow a particular syllabic pattern.

Writing
Explain that haiku is a three-line, unrhymed poem with a special pattern; lines one and three have five syllables, and line two has seven syllables. Write the examples of haiku on the board and mark each syllable. Students choose water fowl to write about—ducks, geese, swans, etc.

Example:

Flying in a V,
The Canada geese head south.
Winter is coming!

Autumn's in the air.
The snow geese honk overhead
On their long journey.

Near the shallow pond,
Fluffy yellow ducks waddle
Behind their mother.

A silent swimmer,
The beautiful white swan looks
At its reflection.

Responding
Students share their haiku with their response groups. Members make positive comments and suggestions for improvements.

Revising/Editing
The author makes changes to improve his/her poem. Then, the peer groups check one anothers' poems for the correct syllabic patterns.

Postwriting
Each student makes a final copy of his/her poem.

Evaluating
The student wrote a three-line poem following the haiku pattern. The student produced a legible copy of the poem.

Extending Writing
Study Japanese culture, history, and people. Write a report about a favorite topic.

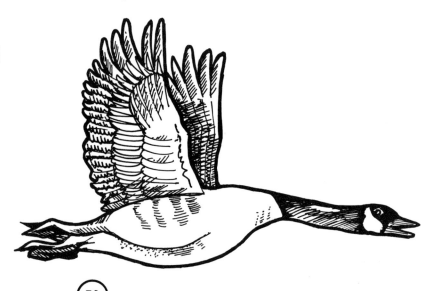

Diamante

Developing Skills
Students will contrast two topics, following the form for a diamante poem. Students will use nouns, adjectives, and participles.

Resource
The Random House Book of Poetry for Children, edited by Jack Prelutsky

Prewriting
Read several selections from **The Random House Book of Poetry for Children** about city life such as Marci Ridlon's "City, City," Jack Prelutsky's "City, Oh City," Langston Hughes' "City Lights," and Lois Lenski's "Sing a Song of People." Then, share some poems about country life.

Writing
At the next class session, have each student write **City** in the center of the top line of his/her paper. Brainstorm and list adjectives on a chart that describe the city. The student chooses two of them for the second line. Then, record the students' suggestions for **-ing** words that relate to the city. Each student writes three participles centered on the third line. The fourth line should begin with two nouns that relate to the city. Save the papers.

At the next writing session, brainstorm nouns, participles, and adjectives relating to country life. Return student papers from the previous session. Students begin on line four and write two nouns relating to the country. Line five lists three **-ing** words. Line six has two adjectives and line seven has the word **Country**.

Diamante Pattern
Example:

one noun
two adjectives
three participles
two nouns/two nouns
three participles
two adjectives
one noun

City vs. Country
City
Big, busy
Hustling, bustling, hurrying
Skyscrapers, factories, barns, meadows
Planting, growing, harvesting
Quiet, green
Country

Responding
Students share their poems in peer groups. Students respond positively to the poems and make suggestions for improving them.

Revising/Editing
Authors make any necessary revisions. They meet in response groups again to check one anothers' poems to make certain that the pattern has been followed.

Postwriting
Students copy their poems neatly on a clean sheet of paper.

Evaluating
The student compares city life and country life with appropriate vocabulary in a diamante poem.

Extending Writing
Have students compare night and day, youth and age, or two characters from a story in a diamante poem.

Name _____

Don't Do It!

Think of all the things that your parents, teachers, or others have told you not to do. Make a list of these in the space below.

Now read through your list. Do you see any items which seem to be grouped together in a natural way? For example, all the things you hear at school, things you hear at home, or maybe a chronological order starting with things you heard as a baby progressing as you have grown up. Underline or highlight the items on your list you would like to group together. Next, think of a good beginning line to introduce your list and a good closing line to finish it. Write your poem here (opening line - list - closing line).

Don't

Read your poem to someone.

Try the same things starting with this phrase: I like . . . .

Name _____

The Name of the Game

Write the letters of your name down the side of the page. For each letter think of a word or phrase to describe yourself.

Example:
Meet Melissa
Everyone's friend
Loves to read
Interested in animals
Sincere
Sometimes likes sports
Also known as Missy.

Design the border to tell about you (favorite colors, hobbies, etc.).

Name _____

30-Minute Ode to a Familiar Object

1. (Five minutes) Go outside and find an object: pretty stone, feather, shell, piece of bark, snakeskin, leaf, flower, etc.

2. (Five minutes) Write words and phrases to describe the object. Use similes when applicable (white as snow, soft as a baby).

3. (Ten Minutes) Think about a memory this object reminds you of (skipping stones in a lake on a camping trip). Write about that memory.

4. (Ten Minutes) Using words and phrases from the above activity, write an ode to the object. Use this form: You are . . . . You remind me of . . . .

Name _____

Once upon a Time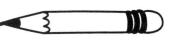

Cut out the cards below. Place all the character cards in one envelope, the setting cards in another, the conflict cards in another, and the object cards in another. Draw one card out of each envelope and use the information on each card in a story.

Character	Setting	Conflict	Object
princess	the moon	attacked by a vicious animal	knife
11-year-old boy	a castle	someone is lost	ball
basketball player	a school	a fight with a friend	UFO
an alien	a house	something has been stolen	horse
an old hermit	the woods	a big game between rival teams	frying pan
grandmother	a deserted island	a race	mug
11-year-old girl	city	someone has disappeared	flashlight
knight in shining armor	farm	search for a buried treasure	shovel
sea captain	inside of an Egyptian pyramid	a mysterious sound	telephone
villain	a cave	something burned	book
wizard	a mountain	moved to a new place	hat

Name _____

Who's the Real Bad Guy?

There is an Indian myth about six blind men who each tried to describe an elephant by feeling only one part. The one who felt the tail was sure an elephant looked like a rope. The one who felt the legs was certain it was like a tree trunk, and so it went. Each had a different point of view and was unable to imagine the elephant from another point of view. We often get caught in the same rut of seeing only one point of view. It is interesting to try to see something from a different perspective.

From whose point of view are each of these stories usually told?

1. "Jack and the Beanstalk" _____
2. "Little Red Riding Hood" _____
3. "Three Bears" _____
4. "Three Little Pigs" _____
5. "Cinderella" _____
6. "Three Billy Goats Gruff" _____

Think about how each of these stories would be different if it was told from the "bad" guy's point of view.

Choose one of these or another familiar fairy tale. List the parts of the story that would change.

Write a new fairy tale based on this different perspective.

Name _____

And They Lived Happily Ever After

This story-writing activity has a cast of two to five people. The first person writes the beginning of the story. After five to seven minutes, pass the paper on to the next person, who continues the story. Again, after five to seven minutes, pass the paper on to the next person, and continue in this way until the last person writes the ending to the story. Read the stories out loud.

_____

_____

_____

_____

_____

_____

_____

_____

_____

_____

_____

_____

_____

_____

_____

_____

_____

_____

_____

_____

_____

_____

Story Starters

The spacecraft landed in my yard . . . .

Everybody liked the kid with the green ears . . . .

The extraterrestrial had powers to . . . .

Vocabulary

sighting
alien
intelligent life
civilizations
communication
galaxies
spacecraft
science fiction
flying saucer
Unidentified Flying Objects
United States Air Force
zoom   flashes   noises

Facts and Fun

Write a newspaper article that describes the sighting and landing of a UFO and the meeting of humans with beings from outer space.

Design a new world and tell where it is located in the universe. Create beings for this world and describe the creatures and their habitats.

Pretend you were an ambassador of the earth and were in charge of showing a visiting space creature around the world. Write about the things you would show it and tell why.

UFOs

Fold this sheet in half horizontally and then into quarters vertically to form a thematic booklet of various fun activities. Then cut this bottom portion off.

Vocabulary

parent
extended family
grandparents
aunts   uncles
cousins
celebrations
rules
sibling   brother   sister
chores   responsibility
reunions
traditions
sharing

Story Starters

When I woke up, I was shocked to discover I had become my mom . . . .

I was supposed to complete all my chores before Dad got home from work. He will be home in 15 minutes and I haven't started yet . . . .

This family reunion was certainly unusual . . . .

Facts and Fun

Make a list of your family rules. Then make up a list of rules you would have if you were a parent.

Think about a book you have read or a TV show or movie you have seen about a family that you really liked. Write a story based on that family.

Study the genealogy of your family. Make a family tree dating back as far as you can.

Family

Fold this sheet in half horizontally and then into quarters vertically to form a thematic booklet of various fun activities. Then cut this bottom portion off.

Vocabulary

Ocelot
American crocodile
Grizzly bear
California condor
Florida panther
Thick-billed parrot
Northern spotted owl
Steller's sea lion
Whooping crane
Bald eagle

Story Starters

I'm raising the last known pair of . . . .

A thick-billed parrot swoops down into our backyard every night at midnight . . . .

The Florida panther pricked its ear at the strange sounds nearby . . . .

Facts and Fun

Tell how littering, insecticides, and fires affect animals' habitats.

Write a letter to your representative in Congress asking for laws to be passed to protect animals.

Using resources at the library, make a list of other endangered animals. Write about what is being done to protect one of these animals.

Endangered Animals

Fold this sheet in half horizontally and then into quarters vertically to form a thematic booklet of various fun activities. Then cut this bottom portion off.

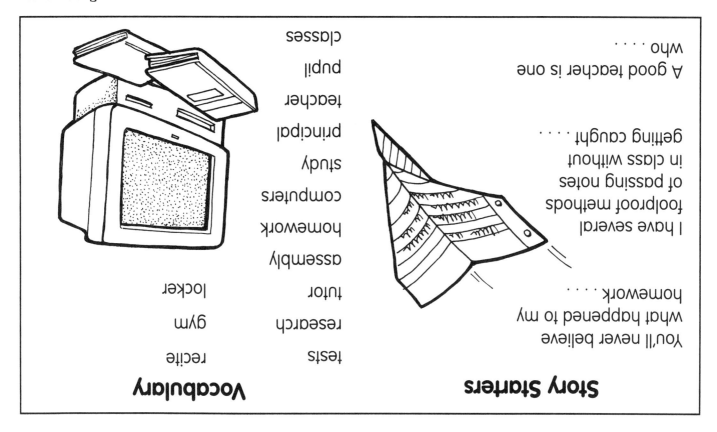

Vocabulary

recite
tests
gym
research
locker
tutor
assembly
homework
computers
study
principal
teacher
pupil
classes

Story Starters

"A good teacher is one who . . . ."

"I have several foolproof methods of passing notes in class without getting caught . . . ."

"You'll never believe what happened to my homework . . . ."

Facts and Fun

Select three careers you think you might enjoy. Research to find out the educational requirements, qualifications, duties, and salary for each.

Interview school employees, such as the nurse, a cook, a teacher, and the custodian. Make a newsletter using the information you gather.

What things do you think should be taught in school that are not? Tell why.

Back to School

Fold this sheet in half horizontally and then into quarters vertically to form a thematic booklet of various fun activities. Then cut this bottom portion off.

Vocabulary

roller coaster
bumper cars
water rides
stuffed animals
candied apples
balloons
dizzy
queasy
monorail
crowds
fun house
Ferris wheel
carousel
cotton candy
arcade games

Story Starters

In the House of Mirrors, I saw a face staring back at me that was not my own . . . .

There was a most unusual prize awarded at the ringtoss game . . . .

We were stranded in the top car of the Ferris wheel . . . .

Facts and Fun

Interview a few adults to find out how amusement parks have changed over the years. Write about the changes.

Design a new ride for an amusement park. Write about and illustrate it.

Tally your friends' favorite amusement park foods. Use this information to design a menu, using catchy names.

Amusement Park

Fold this sheet in half horizontally and then into quarters vertically to form a thematic booklet of various fun activities. Then cut this bottom portion off.

Name _____

The Latest Greatest Breakfast Cereal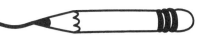

1. Invent a new breakfast cereal. Describe what it looks like, how it tastes, what happens when you pour on the milk, or anything else unique about it.

2. Design the box for your cereal so that people will notice it on a shelf in the grocery store.

3. Plan a newspaper or magazine advertisement to sell your cereal. You might want to include a coupon to encourage people to buy it.

Name _____

Free Writing

There are always thoughts passing through your mind; it's never empty. Free writing helps you put your thoughts on paper. Write nonstop for 10 minutes and record anything that comes to mind. Sometimes what you write during a free writing will be useful for another writing assignment. Do not stop to correct, edit, or revise it. Like anything else, it gets easier with practice. Set a timer for ten minutes and start writing. Have fun.

_____

_____

_____

_____

_____

_____

_____

_____

_____

_____

_____

_____

_____

_____

_____

_____

_____

_____

_____

_____

_____

_____

_____

Name _____

Fair Share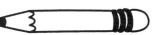

Robinson Middle School has 540 students. The principal, Ms. Staycalm, is making plans for an orderly year.

1. There are 18 classrooms. What will be the average number of students in each?
   _____

2. In each classroom there are six tables. How many students would have to sit at each one?
   _____

3. The school has 144 erasers to divide among the classrooms. How many will each room get?
   _____

4. Only ⅔ of the classrooms have an outside window.
   How many classrooms have an outside window? _____
   How many students must be in a classroom without a window? _____

5. Ms. Staycalm ordered additional computer equipment at a cost of $6,400.00. Students will sell zucchini bread that they make themselves for $2.50 a loaf. How many loaves will each student need to sell to earn the needed money?
   _____

6. Every third student at Robinson is a female.
   How many females are there? _____
   How many students are male? _____

7. Ms. Staycalm asked the students to vote on a mascot. Half of them voted for a pot-bellied pig, ⅜ voted for a chihuahua and 2/16 voted for a goat.
   How many votes did each mascot receive? _____
   Which animal won? _____

EXTENSION

Ms. Staycalm's 6th-grade daughter wanted to save $129.00 for a video game. She earned $5.00 each week for doing chores around the house and $10.00 every other week for mowing a neighbor's lawn. How long will it take her to save enough money for the video game? _____

Name _____

Monkey in the Middle

Circle the fraction whose value is neither greatest nor least in each group

1. $\frac{1}{4}$ $\frac{1}{3}$ $\frac{1}{2}$

2. $\frac{6}{10}$ $\frac{9}{10}$ $\frac{3}{10}$

3. $\frac{4}{5}$ $\frac{4}{12}$ $\frac{4}{8}$

4. $\frac{7}{8}$ $\frac{1}{4}$ $\frac{2}{6}$

5. $\frac{3}{10}$ $\frac{5}{100}$ $\frac{2}{5}$

6. $\frac{7}{14}$ $\frac{5}{8}$ $\frac{3}{4}$

7. $\frac{8}{9}$ $\frac{3}{8}$ $\frac{8}{12}$

8. $\frac{2}{5}$ $\frac{2}{3}$ $\frac{1}{2}$

9. $\frac{5}{6}$ $\frac{1}{4}$ $\frac{7}{8}$

10. $\frac{11}{12}$ $\frac{7}{10}$ $\frac{2}{6}$

11. $\frac{3}{8}$ $\frac{3}{16}$ $\frac{5}{5}$

12. $\frac{2}{12}$ $\frac{3}{4}$ $\frac{7}{14}$

13. $\frac{4}{10}$ $\frac{3}{6}$ $\frac{5}{8}$

14. $\frac{1}{9}$ $\frac{5}{8}$ $\frac{4}{5}$

15. $\frac{2}{3}$ $\frac{7}{8}$ $\frac{2}{8}$

16. $\frac{4}{6}$ $\frac{2}{6}$ $\frac{3}{3}$

17. $\frac{3}{4}$ $\frac{5}{7}$ $\frac{3}{10}$

18. $\frac{1}{3}$ $\frac{1}{4}$ $\frac{9}{10}$

19. $\frac{2}{10}$ $\frac{2}{3}$ $\frac{2}{5}$

20. $\frac{5}{6}$ $\frac{4}{5}$ $\frac{1}{2}$

IF8679 A Little Bit of Everything

Name _____

Doing Decimals

Compute these problems.

1. 14.8 +23.6 **L**	2. 35.2 +1.08 **A**	3. 9.8 +64.9 **D**	4. 0.63 +4.9 **G**	

5. 124.6 +65.08 **L**	6. 42.0 −9.63 **H**	7. 2.1 −0.84 **E**	8. 135.07 −57.92 **D**

9. 88.04 -79.87 **E**	10. 4.7 -3.99 **H**

11. 0.13 + 89.99 = _____ A

12. 61.9 + 14.75 = _____ E

13. 0.91 + 0.34 = _____ E

14. 23.19 + 14.07 = _____ S

15. 104.02 + 79.86 = _____ L

16. 92.01 + 157.9 = _____ O

17. 0.08 + 5.62 = _____ L

18. 300.90 - 158.28 = _____ P

19. 217.5 - 68.92 = _____ O

20. 129.04 - 73.35 = _____ N

21. 6.008 - 5.96 = _____ T

22. 52.195 - 4.067 = _____ A

23. 7.55 - 4.9 = _____ A

Use the letters above to complete a famous quote. Begin with the letter corresponding to the smallest figure and continue until all 23 figures are in order from least to greatest.

" ___ ___ ___   ___ ___ ___ ___ ___   ___ ___ ___   ___ ___ ___ ___ ___ ___ ___ ." - ___ ___ ___ ___ ___ ___

IF8679 A Little Bit of Everything

Name _____

Shopping for Soccer Supplies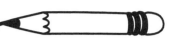

The soccer team members needed to buy their own shin guards, socks, shoes, and shorts. A couple of the players volunteered to do some comparative shopping to find the store with the best deal. Use their charts to answer the questions below.

SPORTS CORNER
Socks ....3 pairs for $9.30
Shoes ....2 pairs for $48.24
Shin Guards..........4 pairs for $32.48
Shorts ....5 pairs for $60.30

JOE'S SOCCER
Socks ....2 pairs for $6.84
Shoes ....3 pairs for $84.15
Shin Guards ....5 pairs for $35.70
Shorts ....4 pairs for $36.36

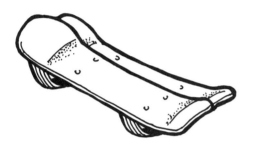  

1. Which store had the best price for socks? How much less were they per pair?

   _____
   _____

2. Which store had the best price for shin guards? How much would you save per pair?

   _____
   _____

3. How much would one pair of shoes and socks cost at Joe's Soccer? How much at Sports Corner?

   _____
   _____

4. Which store had the best price for shorts? How much less were they per pair?

   _____
   _____

5. Total the price per pair for each item at each store. If you could shop at only one store, which one would give you the best overall deal? How much would you save?

   _____
   _____

EXTENSION

If you needed to buy shoes, socks, shin guards, and shorts for a team of 19, using the best price for each item, what would your total cost be? _____

Name _____

Patterns Plus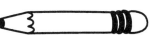

Look for the patterns and fill in the blanks. Describe in words the patterns you see.

1. 3   9   15   21   ___   ___   ___
Description: _____

2. ___   801   702   603   ___   ___   ___
Description: _____

3. 16   24   32   ___   ___   ___   ___
Description: _____

4. ___   82   73   64   ___   ___   ___
Description: _____

5. 2   5   9   14   ___   ___   ___
Description: _____

6. 203   304   405   ___   ___   ___   ___
Description: _____

7. 95   ___   85   ___   ___   70   ___
Description: _____

8. 22   ___   34   ___   46   ___   ___
Description: _____

9. ___   ___   8   16   ___   64   ___
Description: _____

10. 28   36   ___   ___   60   ___   ___
Description: _____

11. 14   23   31   38   ___   ___   ___
Description: _____

12. 4   6   10   18   ___   ___   ___
Description: _____

Name _____

Money Matters

Find the different combinations of $5 and $10 bills you need to make the following: amounts.

Example:
Total $50

# of $5 Bills	0	2	4	6	8	10
# of $10 Bills	5	4	3	2	1	0

1. Total $60

# of $5 Bills	0						
# of $10 Bills	6	5	4	3	2	1	0

2. Total $65

# of $5 Bills	1						
# of $10 Bills	6	5	4	3	2	1	0

3. Total $70

# of $5 Bills	0							
# of $10 Bills	7							

4. Total $75

# of $5 Bills	1							
# of $10 Bills	7							

5. Total $95

# of $5 Bills	1								
# of $10 Bills	9								

6. Total $125

# of $5 Bills	1									
# of $10 Bills	12	11	10	9	8					

Challenge: Find the different combinations of 5-, 10-, and 20-dollar bills you would need for the following amount. There are 36 combinations.

Total $100

# $5	0			
# $10	0			
# $20	5	4	4	4

Name _____

All Primed Up

Cross out the boxes that contain prime numbers. Write the remaining letters in order to answer the riddle.

31 H	5 U	18 B	9 E	29 M	3 S
19 D	4 C	67 N	59 I	35 A	42 U
83 R	112 S	129 E	53 P	81 H	37 D
93 E	101 K	51 W	23 E	147 A	100 S
17 U	77 O	7 S	39 F	89 I	87 F
57 B	79 A	2 T	13 S	105 A	61 E
107 N	11 O	49 S	41 T	22 E	43 L

Riddle: Why did the base stealer fail his sports examination?

Answer: _____

Name _____

Percent Pro

Find the given percentage of the numbers indicated below. Use a calculator if you wish.

Example: 70% of 9 = ?
0.70 x 9 = 6.3

1. 64% of 500   = ___
2. 11% of 80   = ___
3. 35% of 120   = ___
4. 85% of 480   = ___
5. 29% of 50   = ___
6. 9% of 20   = ___
7. 5% of 2,000 = ___
8. 40% of 200   = ___
9. 12% of 95   = ___
10. 70% of 150   = ___

11. 18% of 700   = ___
12. 10% of 160   = ___
13. 75% of 90   = ___
14. 26% of 260   = ___
15. 7% of 40   = ___
16. 5% of 80   = ___
17. 85% of 40   = ___
18. 55% of 450   = ___
19. 2% of 30   = ___
20. 95% of 60   = ___

In the box below, cross out the answers from above. Read the remaining letters to answer the question:

Who invented the ball-point pen in 1943? _____

67.5	42	27	126	80	5.4	4	320	67.6	1.8
A	B	L	D	E	A	N	M	C	F

57	14.5	105	60	206.8	11.4	247.5	94	350	8.8
I	W	R	Z	L	A	E	O	B	N

9.0	100	34	2.8	116	0.6	408	52	16
I	K	S	L	R	I	N	O	T

78

Name _____

Savemore National Bank

In order to teach the concept of interest to his class, Mr. Savemore set up an imaginary bank in his classroom. Each student was given play money which they could put into a savings account. Mr. Savemore then assigned a monthly interest or loan rate to each student to use in his/her calculations.

1. Samantha deposited $12.35 into her savings account. She was given 8% as her monthly rate of interest. Figure how much Samantha would earn in interest at the end of one month. _____
   What would her savings balance be at the beginning of her second month?_____

2. David deposited $18.93. He was assigned an 11% monthly interest rate. What interest would David receive his first month? _____
   What would his adjusted total be with the interest figured in? _____

3. Jennifer started her savings account with $9.18 at an interest rate of 12% monthly. Figure what her balance would be at the end of...
   a. one month. _____
   b. two months. _____
   c. three months. _____

4. Jeremy decided he would borrow $123.00 for a new mountain bike. His interest rate on the 3-year loan was 18% per year. How much would he pay in interest for this loan? _____

5. Susie wanted to borrow $89.95 for a CD player. The rate of interest on her 1½-year loan was 17% per year.
   How much would she pay in interest?   _____
   In total, how much would her CD player cost?   _____

EXTENSION
Choose an amount of money to open an imaginary savings account. Use an 8% monthly interest rate to figure how much you would have at the end of the year.

Name _____

Paper Drive

Miller Middle School held a paper drive to raise money for computers. Work each problem to find out how well each class and the teachers fared during the drive.

_____ 1. The three sixth-grade classes earned $87.00, $72.00, and $96.00 during the paper drive. What was the average amount earned by a sixth-grade class?

_____ 2. The seventh-grade classes tried their best to out-do the sixth-grade classes. They earned $94.00, $88.00, and $76.00. What was their class average?
_____ Did they beat the sixth grade?
_____ If so, by how much?

_____ 3. Not to be out-done by the youngest of the school, the eighth graders really put on the steam. They earned $79.00, $98.00, and $84.00. What was their average?
_____ How much larger was their average than the seventh grade's?
_____ How much larger was it than the sixth grade's?

_____ 4. Find the school's class average using the information from problems 1, 2, and 3.

_____ 5. The teachers also wanted to get into the act. The three sixth-grade teachers earned $74.00, $66.00, and $58.00. What was their individual average?

_____ 6. Did the seventh-grade teachers beat the sixth-grade teachers with earnings of $63.00, $57.00, and $78.00?
_____ What was their individual average?

_____ 7. The eighth-grade teachers collected $58.00, $69.00, and $92.00. What was their individual average?

EXTENSION

Find the school average for classes and teachers using the above information.

Name _____

School Property Dimensions

Mr. Solve-It's class measured the school and the school grounds when solving problems dealing with area, perimeter, and volume.

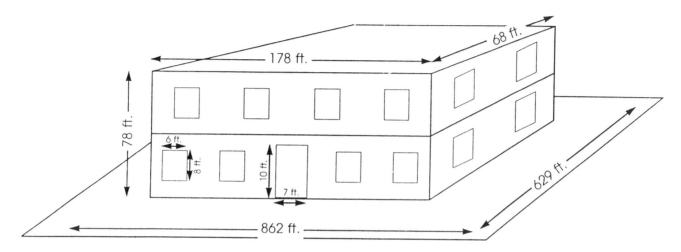

1. What is the perimeter of the building? _____

2. What is the area of the roof of the building? _____

3. What is the area of the front door? _____

4. What is the area of a window? _____

5. There are the same number of windows on the other two sides of the school. If glass for the windows costs $8.25 a square foot, how much would it cost to replace the glass in all the windows? _____

6. What is the perimeter of the property? _____

7. What is the area of the property? _____

8. What portion of the property is not used for the school building? _____

9. What is the volume of the school building? _____

EXTENSION
Find the dimensions of your school and its property. Work each problem using those figures.

Name _____

Choko Airlines . . . Dogtown Airport

Arrival			Departure		
Flight #	Time	From	Flight #	Time	Destination
011	7:15 A.M.	Boston	003	6:50 A.M.	Nashville
274	7:47 A.M.	St. Louis	108	7:24 A.M.	Athens
314	8:02 A.M.	Bangor	960	7:40 A.M.	Dallas
366	8:27 A.M.	Denver	274	8:15 A.M.	Grand Rapids
411	9:10 A.M.	Chicago	304	9:00 A.M.	Boston
438	9:32 A.M.	Paris	419	9:40 A.M.	Ogden
512	9:55 A.M.	Toronto	450	10:10 A.M.	Denver
560	10:24 A.M.	Nashville	321	10:54 A.M.	Milwaukee

Use the schedule to answer the questions below.

1. It's 6:30 A.M. How long must Jean wait for his cousin Fifi to arrive from Paris?

   _____

2. Carlos is on flight 274 from St. Louis to Grand Rapids. How long must he wait in Dogtown? _____

3. The flight to Athens takes 6 hours and 40 minutes. When should Dimitri arrive in Athens (Dogtown time)? _____

4. What is the difference between arrival from Bangor and departure to Milwaukee?

   _____

5. Paula Veer loves air travel. She arrives from and returns to Boston every morning for fun. The flight takes 2 hours and 15 minutes each way. How long can Paula Veer expect to be gone from Boston each day? _____

6. Today Stu is flying to Denver on business. His wife, Ty, is flying back from Denver this morning. What is the most time they can share in the morning? _____

7. It is 5:30 A.M. Melvis is off to Nashville to make a name for himself. How long must he wait? _____

8. Buck arrived in Dogtown from Chicago. Next, he's off to Ogden. How long must he wait? _____

9. Roy knows the flight to Dallas takes 3 hours and 40 minutes. When will he arrive there (Dogtown time)? _____

Name _____

Calculate This! ━━━━━━━━━━━━━━━━━━━━━━━━▷

Use your calculator to solve the following problems.

1. At Burger Queen, Bucky Smidt looked at the menu:
   hamburger $0.89
   chili dog $0.85
   cola (s, m, l) $0.51, $0.74, $0.97
   chips $0.31
   Burger Princess Supreme $1.48

   Bucky spent $4.12, without tax, on five items. Exactly what did he buy? (Hint: He bought two of one item.)

2. Using eight of the digits 1-9 each once, write the equation with . . .

   a. the largest difference. _____

   b. the smallest difference. _____

   c. the largest sum. _____

   d. the smallest sum. _____

   e. the largest product. _____

   f. the smallest product. _____

   g. the largest quotient. _____

   h. the smallest quotient (greater than one). _____

3. Herman went to the pet shop where he bought an eel and a guppy for $3.20. The eel cost $2.00 more than the guppy. How much was the guppy? _____

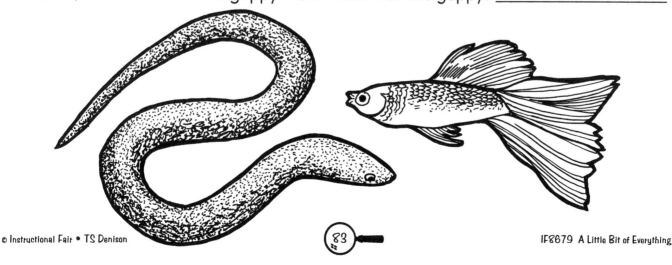

Name _____

Do As the Romans Do

The ancient Romans developed a system of numerals which is quite different from the one we use today.

I	II	III	IV	V	VI	VII	VIII	IX	X	XI	XII	XIII	XIV	XV
1	2	3	4	5	6	7	8	9	10	11	12	13	14	15

XVI	XVII	XVIII	XIX	XX	XXX	XL	L	C	D	M
16	17	18	19	20	30	40	50	100	500	1,000

Look for a pattern in the way the numerals are formed. Based on that pattern how would you write these in Roman numerals?

23 _____   17 _____   1,111 _____

44 _____   68 _____   575 _____

52 _____   99 _____   946 _____

Solve these problems.

1. XVIII + XXII = _____

2. VI + XIX = _____

3. M – CC = _____

4. LXXXIV – XLII = _____

5. VI • XI = _____

6. X • V • I = _____

7. C ÷ XX = _____

8. XC ÷ VI = _____

9. XLIV + XXXIX = _____

10. DCLXXII + CCCXCI = _____

11. D – CLXV = _____

12. C – XX = _____

13. XV • V = _____

14. VIII • XXX = _____

15. MM ÷ L = _____

16. XLII ÷ VII = _____

17. Why do you think we don't continue to use the Roman numeral system today?

_____

Name _____

Weather Graphing

Graphs have a **vertical axis** and a **horizontal axis.** The axes are labeled to show what is being compared.

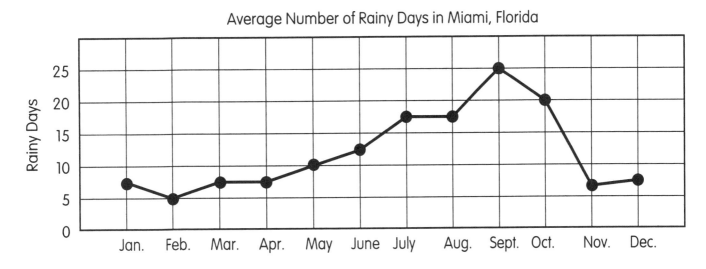

Average Number of Rainy Days in Miami, Florida

Using the data plotted on the graph, answer the following questions.

1. What is the title of the graph? _____

2. How is the vertical axis labeled? _____

3. What is contained in the horizontal axis? _____

4. Which month had the greatest number of rainy days?_____

5. Which two-month period shows the greatest change in the number of rainy days?
   _____

6. Which month was the driest? _____

7. Based on this graph, which two months should have been the best for tourists?
   Explain. _____

Using the graph, fill in the blanks below. (Hint: when finding the median of an even number of numerals, divide by two the sum of the two numerals in the middle.)

8. range: _____   9. mean: _____   10. median: _____   11. mode: _____

Name _____

Compiling Data

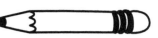

Use the following information and the boxes to create three bar graphs. Make certain to label the vertical axis, the horizontal axis, and title each graph.

1. 1993 State Populations

North Dakota	640,000
Vermont	560,000
Montana	800,000
Wyoming	450,000

2. Income per Capita

State A	$9,120
State B	$9,460
State C	$6,580
State D	$8,980

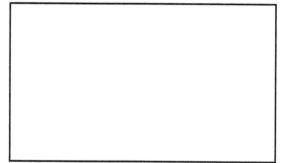

3. Heights of Garden Flowers

Daisy	3 feet 6 inches
Yarrow	2 feet
Peony	3 feet
Hollyhock	6 feet
Cone flower	3 feet

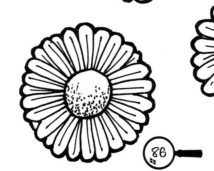

Name _____

Compiling Data II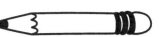

Use the following information and the boxes to create three line graphs. Make certain to label the vertical axis, the horizontal axis, and title each graph.

1. High temperatures for July 1 - 7:

Mon.	78°
Tues.	88°
Wed.	92°
Thurs.	96°
Fri.	96°
Sat.	98°
Sun.	92°

2. Cars sold in 1994:

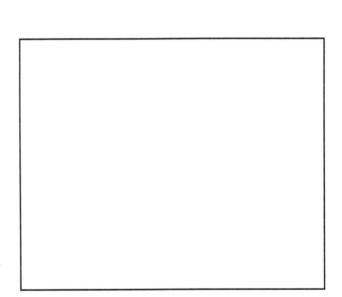

Jan.	86
Feb.	143
Mar.	135
Apr.	152
May	201
Jun.	270
Jul.	186
Aug.	157
Sept.	164
Oct.	169
Nov.	135
Dec.	101

3. Meteor count for one week:

Mon.	17
Tues.	3
Wed.	0
Thurs.	7
Fri.	9
Sat.	8
Sun.	11

Name _____

A Slice of the Pie

Mr. Ambitious' class earned $482.00 during the school year in order to purchase new books for the library. The graph shows what percentage of the money was earned from each activity. Use the graph to answer the questions.

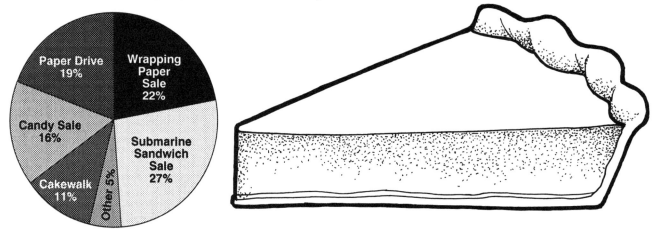

1. Which fundraiser earned the most money? _____

   How much money did it make? $ _____

2. How much money was earned selling candy? $ _____

3. How much money was earned from the cakewalk? $ _____

4. How much more did the class earn from
   the candy sale than from the cakewalk? $ _____

5. How much money was made selling wrapping paper? $ _____

6. How much money did the class earn from the paper drive? $ _____

7. How much less was earned on the paper drive
   than from the wrapping paper sale? $ _____

EXTENSION

Make a pie graph showing percentages of the following information from a bake sale held the following year.

Goods Sold	350 items
Cupcakes	30
Layer Cakes	15
Brownies	35
Carrot Cakes	20
Oatmeal Cookies	100
Chocolate Chip Cookies	150

Name _____

A New Mall?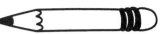

City Hall is considering a proposal to build a new shopping mall in a wooded area within the city boundaries. Before it is put to a vote, City Hall decided to run a survey. Out of 4,250 residents and 182 local businesses, 1,000 people were surveyed. The results are graphed below.

Based on the information in the graph, answer the following questions.

1. Should the mall be built? Explain.

_____

_____

2. Give two reasons why City Hall should vote in favor of the shopping mall proposal.

_____

_____

3. Give two reasons why City Hall should vote against the shopping mall proposal.

_____

_____

4. What is the mean of the percentage of people who voted yes on the three questions?

_____

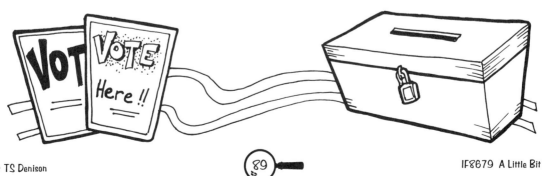

Name _____

Ordered Pairs

Answer each riddle by writing the letters of the
points on the graph in the same order as
the ordered pairs.

1. **Riddle:** What occurs once in every minute, twice in every moment, but not once in a
   thousand years?
   (-4, +2), (-3,-1), (-2, -4) (-1, +1), (-2, -4), (-4, +2), (-4, +2), (-2, -4), (0, 0) (1, -3)

   _____

2. **Riddle:** What gets wetter as it dries?
   (+2, +2), (+3, -3), (+2, +2), (-2, -4), (0, 0) (-4, +2), (+4, +2), (+3, +5), (-2, -4), (-1, +1)

   _____

3. **Riddle:** What five-letter word has six left when you take away two?
   (+5, +3), (+6, -2), (-5, -4), (-4, +2), (-6, +4)

   _____

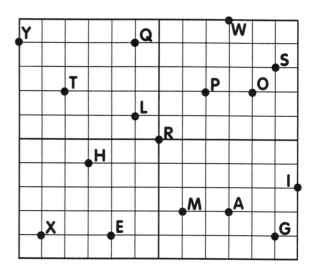

Name _____

Freezing Temperatures

Mrs. Fahrenheit taught the class to add and subtract integers using the class thermometer and the week's changing temperatures.

1. When the class arrived at school, the thermometer registered –3°F. It later rose 8°F, and then dropped 6°F by the end of the school day. What was the temperature at the end of the school day?

   _____

2. The next day was much warmer. It started at +12°F. By noon it had risen 41°. A storm blew in that afternoon and the temperature quickly dropped 30°. What was the final temperature?

   _____

3. The storm was responsible for a very low temperature the following morning. It was –12°F, then it dropped 8° more, rose 15°, then dropped again 4°. What was the final temperature?

   _____

4. The students were happy to see 28°F on Thursday morning. It quickly dropped 5°, then rose 15°, then dropped another 4°, and the day ended with it rising 8°. What was the temperature at the end of the day?

   _____

5. Friday's temperature started at 16°F. It then dropped 3°, rose 21°, dropped 6°, and then rose 4°. What was the ending temperature?

   _____

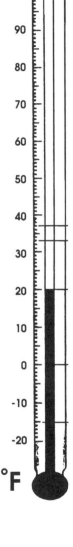

EXTENSION
Create a chart of the temperature changes throughout the day. Indicate the number of degrees it rises and drops every hour.

How Much Is a Liter?

Name _____

Complete each of the activities below to help you understand what the capacity of a liter really is.

1. Take the glass that you usually drink from and pour milk into it. Make certain it is the amount that you normally drink. Measure how many milliliters this is. How many glassfulls will it take for you to drink 1 L? _____ How many liters do you drink each week? _____

2. Turn on your shower. Place the 1 L measuring cup underneath the spigot so that you catch the water coming out. Have someone time how long it takes you to fill 1 L. How many liters of water do you think you use to take a shower? _____

3. Pour your regular serving of dry cereal into a bowl. Now, measure and pour 200 mL of milk on your cereal. Is this the amount that you normally use? If not, measure and pour on the amount that you regularly use. How many bowlfuls will it take for you to use 1 L of milk on your cereal? _____

4. Fill your bathtub with the amount of water that you normally use. Take your bath. When you are done, measure how many liters of water you use by pouring out into the sink each and every liter of water that you had in the bathtub. How many liters of water do you use to take a bath? _____

5. Measure 1 L of water and place it in a pitcher. Put it in the refrigerator. Whenever you get thirsty, drink some of it. How long did it take you to drink the entire liter? _____ How many liters of water do you think you drink each day? _____ Each week? _____ Each year? _____

6. Wash out a milk carton from your school lunch and fill it with water. Pour the water into the measuring cup. Continue refilling and pouring the water into the cup until you have 1 L. How many filled cartons does it take to equal 1 L? _____ How many cartons of milk do you drink each day? _____ How many liters of milk do you drink each week at school? _____

7. Fill an empty 12 oz. aluminum can with water. Pour it into the 1 L measuring cup. Estimate how many 12 oz. refills it will take to reach 1 L. _____ Now, refill the measuring cup to see how many it really takes. _____ How close were you? _____

8. Find a number of different-sized balloons that you think have the capacity of 1 L. Fill them one at a time to see which ones really have the capacity of 1 L. (Make certain they are filled to a safe amount and will not burst.)

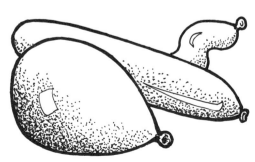

Name _____

Time Can Mean So Much!

Water-saving shower heads now allow 2.5 gallons of water per minute to flow out. 1 gallon = 3.78 L. So, 2.5 x 3.78 = 9.45 L. Therefore 9.45 L of water is flowing out of the shower head per minute.

Determine the quantity of water used for each shower below.

Part One: **When Time Is Given**	Part Two: **When Gallons Are Given**	Part Three: **When Total Liters Are Given**

Example: A two-minute shower
9.45L (liters per minute)
x___2 (number of minutes)
18.90L (total flow of water)
	Example: 5 gallons
	1. Divide: $2.5{\overline{\smash{\big)}\,5}}$ 2
	
	2. 9.45L
	    x___2
	   18.90L (total liters used)
		Example: 18.90 L
		1. Divide: $9.45{\overline{\smash{\big)}\,18.90}}$ 2
		
		2. A two-minute shower

Part One: How Many Liters Were Used?

1. A 5-minute shower

   9.45L
 x___5   ____ L
          Used

2. A 7-minute shower

   9.45L
 x___7   ____ L
          Used

3. A 3-minute shower

   9.45L
 x___3   ____ L
          Used

4. A 9-minute shower

   9.45L
 x___9   ____ L
          Used

Part Two: How Many Liters Were Used?

1. 7.5 gal

           ____ L
$2.5{\overline{\smash{\big)}\,7.5}}$ x____
           ____ L

2. 17.5 gal

           ____ L
$2.5{\overline{\smash{\big)}\,17.5}}$ x____
           ____ L

3. 10 gal

           ____ L
$2.5{\overline{\smash{\big)}\,10}}$ x____
           ____ L

4. 22.5 gal

           ____ L
$2.5{\overline{\smash{\big)}\,22.5}}$ x____
           ____ L

Part Two: How Long Was the Shower?

1. 28.35 L

$9.45{\overline{\smash{\big)}\,28.35}}$

How Long Was the Shower?
_____ min

2. 47.25 L

$9.45{\overline{\smash{\big)}\,47.25}}$

How Long Was the Shower?
_____ min

3. 56.70 L

$9.45{\overline{\smash{\big)}\,56.70}}$

How Long Was the Shower?
_____ min

4. 85.05 L

$9.45{\overline{\smash{\big)}\,85.05}}$

How Long Was the Shower?
_____ min

Name _____

Have You Ever Been On "Metric Road"?

1,000 meters (m) = 1 kilometer (km)

Zoom along the metric road, converting every sign and path to kilometers!

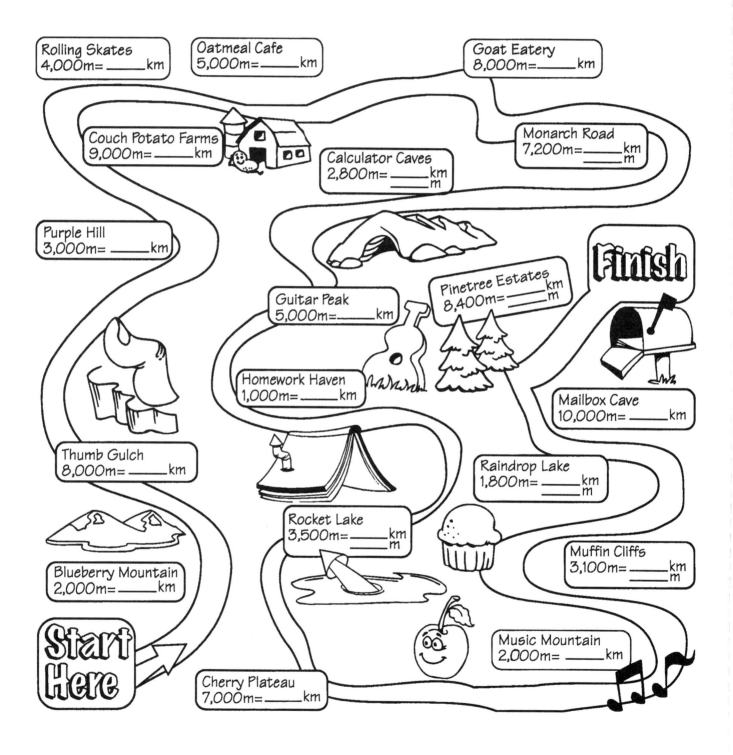

Rolling Skates
4,000m= _____ km

Oatmeal Cafe
5,000m= _____ km

Goat Eatery
8,000m= _____ km

Couch Potato Farms
9,000m= _____ km

Calculator Caves
2,800m= _____ km
_____ m

Monarch Road
7,200m= _____ km
_____ m

Purple Hill
3,000m= _____ km

Guitar Peak
5,000m= _____ km

Pinetree Estates
8,400m= _____ km
_____ m

Finish

Homework Haven
1,000m= _____ km

Mailbox Cave
10,000m= _____ km

Thumb Gulch
8,000m= _____ km

Raindrop Lake
1,800m= _____ km
_____ m

Rocket Lake
3,500m= _____ km
_____ m

Muffin Cliffs
3,100m= _____ km
_____ m

Blueberry Mountain
2,000m= _____ km

Music Mountain
2,000m= _____ km

Start Here

Cherry Plateau
7,000m= _____ km

94

Name _____

Calculator Calculations

Figure how many kilometers it takes to equal the following distances in miles.
Calculate the following problems.

Difference in feet between miles and kilometers	**Difference in distance between 1 mile and 1 kilometer**
5,280 ft (feet in 1 mi)	1.000 (1 mi)
- 3,280.8 ft (feet in 1 km)	- 0.621 (km equivalent of 1 mi)
1,999.2 ft (difference)	0.379 mi (difference)

How many kilometers does it take to
equal at least 1 mi?

Example: 0.621 mi
$$\frac{\times 2}{1.242 \text{ mi}}$$

A km is a little longer than a ½ mile (.621).
2 km = 1.242 miles

How many kilometers does it take to equal at least:

1. 3 mi? _____ km

2. 5 mi? _____ km

3. 10 mi? _____ km

4. 2 mi? _____ km

5. 6 mi? _____ km

6. 4 mi? _____ km

7. 9 mi? _____ km

8. 7 mi? _____ km

9. 12 mi? _____ km

10. 25 mi? _____ km

11. 15 mi? _____ km

12.   8 mi? _____ km

13.   1 mi? _____ km

14. 0.5 mi? _____ km

15. 22 mi? _____ km

16. 50 mi? _____ km

17. 14 mi? _____ km

18. 16 mi? _____ km

Name _____

Challenges to Amaze You!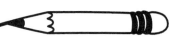

Measure in meters how far you can do the following activities. Round off to the nearest meter.

1. Walk with a basketball being supported by your thumb.

   # of meters _____

2. Hop with one ankle fastened to a friend's ankle.

   # of meters _____

3. Play catch with a balloon filled with water. Move back one step after each successful catch. # of meters _____

4. Place a Ping-Pong ball on a plastic spoon and grip it between your teeth. How far can you jog? # of meters _____

5. Throw a softball backwards over your shoulder. # of meters _____

6. Throw a fistful of cotton balls. # of meters _____

7. Lay down a piece of string in a straight line. See how far you can walk in a straight line with your eyes closed. # of meters _____

8. Throw a walnut using a plastic spoon. # of meters _____

9. Build a castle using empty milk cartons (½-pint cartons from lunch).

   height in meters _____

10. Walk while balancing a math book on your head! # of meters _____

11. Walk balancing a baseball bat on the inside of your palm.

    # of meters _____

12. Hop backwards. # of meters _____

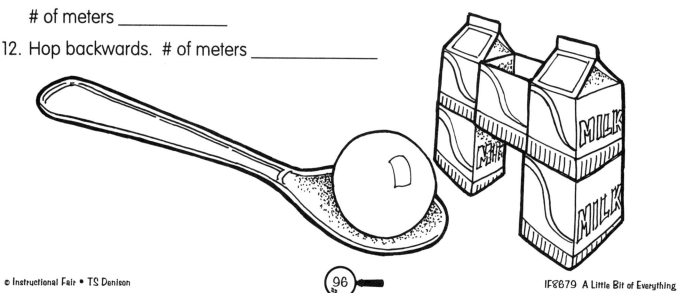

Name _____

Here's a Challenge for You!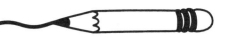

Think about each problem. Diagram or write out the problem and then solve it. Have fun! Take on the challenge!

1. Samuel just realized that each slice of the loaves of bread that he purchased at the store for his parents is 1 cm in width. Also, each loaf contains 25 slices. If the total width of all the loaves is 100 cm, how many loaves are there? _____ How many meters does that total in all?_____

2. Tony's father is laying brick to build a barbeque. Each brick is 5 cm in length. He is leaving a 1 cm width of mortar between each brick. How many bricks will he lay before he reaches a height of 23 cm? (Note: that height does not include any mortar on the top brick.) _____

3. Allison would like to spread six 25-cm-wide chairs across the front porch. She wants to leave 10 cm between each chair. The porch is 2 m, 30 cm wide. Will she have enough room for her guests? _____

   If she sets out three rows of six chairs in each, how many chairs will that be in all?

   _____

4. Jessy, Mark's golden retriever, ran forward 600 cm, then back 100 cm, then forward 200 cm, in order to catch the flying disk in the air! How many meters did Jessy actually move forward?_____

5. Three subs were purchased for the huge picnic that the fifth grade was having to celebrate the opening of their new school. Each sub was 200 cm in length. At the end of the picnic, the first sub was now 30 cm in length, the second 50 cm in length, and the third 40 cm in length. Did they have a total of more or less than 1 meter remaining of submarine sandwich to munch on later? _____ If so, how much more or less than a meter did they have remaining?_____

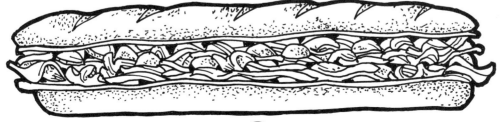

Name _____

Go for the Gold!

You can have a mini Olympics and practice measuring in metrics at the same time. There are five events. Try each one three times and record your scores. You can take your best score in each event or average the three scores together.

1. Straw javelin: Stand at the starting line and throw the straw as far as you can. Measure the distance in centimeters.
2. Eight-inch paper plate discus: Start at the starting line and throw the plate as you would a frisbee. Measure the distance in centimeters.
3. Cotton ball shot put: Stand at the starting line and throw the cotton ball as far as you can. It must stay dry. Measure the distance in centimeters.
4. Penny long jump: Place one penny at the starting line. Use another penny to flick the other like a tiddlywink by pushing down on one edge. Measure the distance from the starting line to the back edge of the penny in centimeters.
5. Paper triangle high jump: Fold a piece of paper into a triangle, like you would fold a flag. Have a friend stand a ruler on the table and hold a pencil at the 10-centimeter line. Stand the triangle on one of its points, holding it with one finger at the top point. With your other hand, flick it up over the pencil. If you cannot make it over, lower the pencil and try again. If you make it over easily, raise the pencil and keep trying until you reach your highest "jump."

	first	second	third	average
straw javelin				
paper plate discus				
cotton ball shot put				
penny long jump				
triangle high jump				

Name _____

Area of Art

Ms. Ringleader's art class built a sculpture for the front of the school. Since it was made entirely of geometric shapes, Mr. Gofigure decided it would be fun to find out its total area. In order to do this, he first had his classes find the area of each piece.

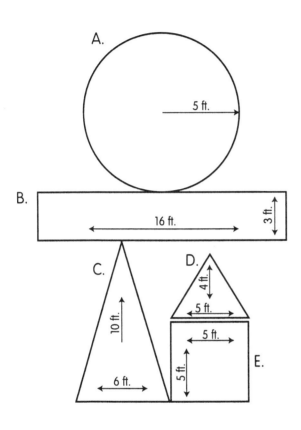

Area: A. _____

B. _____

C. _____

D. _____

E. _____

Total Area: _____

EXTENSION

Increase the lengths of each dimension above by 20%. Find the area of each shape. What is the total area? Is the new area also 20% larger? Explain.

Area: A. _____   B. _____   C. _____   D. _____   E. _____

Total Area: _____

Name _____

Street Sense

Ms. Ima Map used a neighborhood map to help her students understand geometric lines.

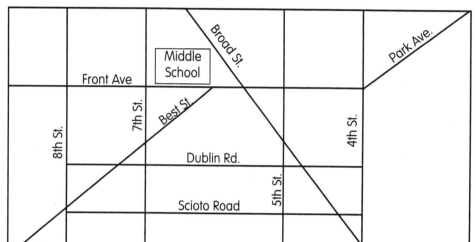 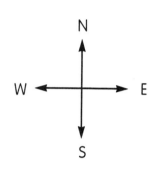

1. Name two streets that run parallel to 5th Street.

   _____

   Name two streets that are not parallel to 5th Street.

   _____

2. Name a street that intersects Scioto Road.

   _____

3. Are Dublin Road and 7th Street perpendicular or parallel to each other?

   _____

4. Does Broad Street intersect Front Avenue or is it parallel to Front?

   _____

5. Name the first street directly south of Front Avenue and parallel to it.

   _____

6. Which street runs perpendicular to 5th Street and is the street farthest south shown on the map?

   _____

7. Which two streets intersect directly west of the school?

   _____

8. Name the three roads that do not run directly north and south or east and west.

   _____

EXTENSION
Draw a map of your immediate area. Determine streets that are parallel and perpendicular.

How Much Will It Cost?

Many students your age have money of their own. You may receive an allowance or earn money babysitting or with a paper route. Using a budget will help you spend your money wisely.

Vocabulary: Budget: a plan for spending money
              Income: the money available
              Expenses: what you want to do with your money
              Deficit: the amount you are short
              Balance: making expenses equal the income

1. Susie receives an allowance of $10.00 a month. She also babysits every Thursday after school and earns $4.00 each week (about 4 weeks a month). Sometimes she can earn more money by doing extra chores or babysitting.

2. Here are some things Susie would like to do with her money: Save some of it in her bank account—$2.50, use some to donate to her class project to buy shoes for homeless children—$2.50, buy a new shirt—on sale this month for $7.00, go to movies with friends—$3.00, buy a Coke and popcorn at the movies—$3.00, buy a birthday present for her Mom—$5.00, buy a book from the school book fair—$4.00, gum and candy—$3.00, souvenir from the class field trip—$2.00. Does Susie have enough income to cover her expenses? Use this chart to help.

Income   Expenses

       _____   _____

       _____   _____

       _____   _____

       _____   _____

       _____   _____

       _____   _____

       _____   _____

       _____   _____

Total: _____   Total: _____

How much is her deficit? (total expenses minus total income) _____

What are two different ways Susie can make her budget balance?

1. _____

2. _____

Name _____

My Budget

Use this form to plan a budget for yourself. It can be real or imaginary. Write the money you have available under "Income" and the ways to spend it under "Expenses."

Income	Expenses

Total _____   Total _____

Is there a deficit (more in the expense column)? _____ If so, how much? _____

Is there a surplus (more in the income column)? _____ If so, how much? _____

What can I do to make my budget balance?

_____

_____

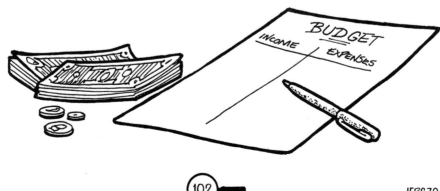

Name _____

Number Wise ～～～～～～～～～～～

Work the equations to find the important numbers. Calculators may be used.

1. Days in a fortnight _____ $[(38 - 20) \div 2] + 5$

2. States in the U.S.A. _____ $(8 + 29 - 12) \times 2$

3. Feet in a mile _____ $(44 + 16) \times 11 \times 8$

4. Years in a decade _____ $(6 \times 9) + 7 - 51$

5. Freezing point of water in Fahrenheit _____ $[(24 \div 4) -4] \times 16$

6. Months in a year _____ $(8 + 8 + 200) \div 18$

7. Feet in a yard _____ $[(4 - 4) \times 5] + 3$

8. Year U.S. declared independence _____ $(4 \times 11 \times 4) + 1,600$

9. Ounces in a pound _____ $(3 \times 8 \times 2) \div 3$

10. Freezing point of water in Celsius _____ $(84 \div 7 \times 3) - 36$

11. Years in a century _____ $(9 - 8 + 3) \times 25$

12. Continents of the world _____ $[(15 - 3) + 30] \div 6$

13. A gross _____ $(48 \div 4) \times 3 \times 4$

14. Quarters in a dollar _____ $(9 - 6) + 5 - 4$

15. Years in a millennium _____ $[(300 + 33) \times 3] + 1$

16. Bits in a byte _____ $5 + 7 + 8 - 12$

17. Hours in a day _____ $(6 \times 3) + 9 - 3$

18. Events in a pentathlon _____ $[(54 \div 3) \div 3] - 1$

19. Sides to a hexagon _____ $(19 + 35 + 12) \div 11$

20. Days in a year _____ $[(1,000 - 1) \div 3] + 32$

Name _____

Mixed-Up Measures

Each scrambled word is a unit of measurement. On the first blank of each line, write each measurement spelled correctly. On the second blank tell what each measures (length, time, distance, etc.). Caution: Some of the units included are not currently as common as they once were.

Example: L I E M   Mile   Distance

1. E C R A   _____   _____

2. T R I M E L O K E   _____   _____

3. T R I L E   _____   _____

4. G A U L E E   _____   _____

5. C N O S E D   _____   _____

6. L A L O N G   _____   _____

7. P R E A M E   _____   _____

8. G R O F L U N   _____   _____

9. A T R A C   _____   _____

10. M I L K G O A R   _____   _____

11. B I C U T   _____   _____

12. R E S H O P R O W E   _____   _____

13. C L I B E E D   _____   _____

14. G E R E D E   _____   _____

15. C A R E T H E   _____   _____

16. H O T M A F   _____   _____

17. P O T O E S A N   _____   _____

18. S L U B E H   _____   _____

Name _____

Nine Square Dare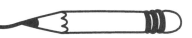

Place a number from 1 to 9 in each empty box so that these patterns are true:
1. Each number 1-9 appears exactly once in each row.
2. Each number 1-9 appears exactly once in each column.
3. Each number 1-9 appears exactly once in each smaller, 3 x 3 square.

1				6		2		5
	3	5	7				1	
	9							
3			5				6	
	2	7			8			
	6						4	
	6	1		5				3
	3		8					
7							5	9

Name _____

Math Maze

Here is the pattern that will get you through this maze: Move one box in any direction (horizontally, vertically, or diagonally) as long as the number is four less or three greater than the number in your current box. Begin with the 3 in the START box.

START 3	7	-6	1	-2	1
-1	6	-2	-5	4	0
2	-5	0	6	3	-1
0	-4	-7	-2	-5	2
3	-1	-6	-9	-6	5
1	-3	2	-1	3	0
5	0	-4	-2	-5	2
2	4	-1	0	3	-2 END

Name _____

Valentine Exchange

At a recent Valentine's Day party, five girls—Abigail, Bethany, Chelsea, Danielle, and Esther—each received one of the valentines shown here. Use the clues, the drawing, and the chart below to help you figure out who received which one.

Clues:
A. Abigail's valentine had lace.
B. Bethany's valentine was from either Eddy or Freddy.
C. Chelsea's valentine did not have an arrow on it.
D. Danielle's valentine had no words on the front.
E. Esther's valentine had no words, no lace, and no arrow.

	Abigail	Bethany	Chelsea	Danielle	Esther
Valentine 1					
Valentine 2					
Valentine 3					
Valentine 4					
Valentine 5					

Answers: Abigail received valentine # _____.
Bethany received valentine # _____.
Chelsea received valentine # _____.
Danielle received valentine # _____.
Esther received valentine # _____.

Name _____

Dinner Winner

Mr. and Mrs. Top are hosting a unique dinner party. Upon arrival, each guest is given a set of clues for the seating arrangement at the dinner table. The first to discover the correct plan wins a fabulous prize. How quickly can you uncover the correct solution?

| window |

Guests

Mr. Top
Mrs. Top
Mr. Bottom
Mrs. Bottom
Mr. Left
Mrs. Left
Mr. Right
Mrs. Right
Mr. Center
Mrs. Center

Clues:

1. Mr. and Mrs. Top, as host and hostess, will occupy the chairs at the ends of the table.

2. Mr. Center will sit between a Left and a Bottom.

3. Mr. Left will sit two seats to the right of Mrs. Bottom.

4. Mrs. Right will sit two seats to the left of Mrs. Left.

5. Mr. Top will sit nearer to the window than his wife.

6. The Tops and the Bottoms are the only ones seated across from their spouses.

7. Mrs. Left will sit to the left of Mr. Bottom who is on Mrs. Top's left.

Write your answers in the diagram above.

Name _____

An Average Class

Here are the names of the 20 students in Ms. Mean's class:

Joel	Josephine	Jill	Jewell
Jerry	Jacqueline	Jimmy	Jasmyne
James	Julia	Jennifer	Jawan
Joshua	Justin	Jasper	Jamal
Janet	Janice	Justus	Jillian

1. What is the mean (average) number of letters in the students' first names? __

2. What number of letters appears most often? _____

Write the first names of the five students in the left-hand column here:

3. Now, add a last name to each first name so that the average number of letters for the first and last names combined is 12.

4. Try to make your own list of first names in which the average number of letters per name is exactly three. Use at least ten names in your list. Make certain at least half of your names do not have three letters.

5. Now, make your own list of last names in which the average number of letters per name is exactly ten. Use at least ten names in your list. Make certain at least half of your names do not have ten letters.

Dated Odds

Name _____

Look at the calendar page page shown here as you answer the following questions. Write your answers as fractions in lowest terms. For example, if the chances of an event happening are 3 out of 30, it would be written as ³⁄₃₀ and then reduced to ¹⁄₁₀.

If you were to close your eyes and randomly point to a date on this calendar page, what is the probability that your finger would land on:

A. Nov. 21? _____

B. a Tuesday? _____

C. a Sunday? _____

D. a weekday? _____

E. a weekend day? _____

F. an even-numbered day? _____

G. a date containing one or more of the digit 2? _____

H. a date containing one 2? _____

I. a date containing two digits? _____

J. a date containing two matching digits? _____

K. a date containing three digits? _____

L. any day of the week that contains the letter S? _____

November						
Sun.	Mon.	Tues.	Wed.	Thurs.	Fri.	Sat.
1	2	3	4	5	6	7
8	9	10	11	12	13	14
15	16	17	18	19	20	21
22	23	24	25	26	27	28
29	30					

Name _____

Paint Point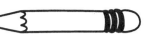

The Tight-Pocket Toy Company has a manufacturing problem. One of their most popular items, THE BLOCKS, is becoming more and more expensive to produce because of the large amount of paint used in coating the blocks.

The company has been dipping each block individually into a tub of paint, coating all sides of each block. Now they are considering dipping groups of blocks so that some sides of some cubes are not painted.

For example, if three blocks (with a total of 18 sides) are arranged like this

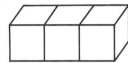

and dipped in paint, there will be four sides in all that will not be painted, thus saving the Tight-Pocket Toy Company a considerable amount of paint and money.

To help the company in its research, try to draw different arrangements with cubes to meet the following requirements. Some may not be possible. If so, write IMPOSSIBLE in the space provided.

1. Four cubes with 6 unpainted sides

2. Four cubes with 7 unpainted sides

3. Four cubes with 8 unpainted sides

4. Five cubes with 8 unpainted sides
   (Try to find 3 different arrangements.)

5. Five cubes with 10 unpainted sides

6. Five cubes with 14 unpainted sides

Name _____

What's My Number?

Use the clues to guess which number is being described.

1. a) it is a multiple of 2, 3, 7, and 8.
   b) it is less than 400
   c) the sum of its digits is 12   _____

2. a) it is a prime number
   b) it is > 500 and <700
   c) the sum of its digits is 11   _____

3. a) it is a perfect square
   b) it contains 3 digits under 5, two are the same
   c) it is a multiple of 2, 4, 6, 8, and 9   _____

4. a) it contains four consecutive numbers
   b) it is less than 6,000
   c) the sum of its digits is 22   _____

5. a) it has four repeating digits
   b) it is a multiple of 2, 3, and 6
   c) it is greater than 4,000   _____

6. a) $\sqrt[3]{343}$
   b) it is a prime number
   c) it is a single-digit number   _____

7. a) reads the same forwards and backwards
   b) if you add or multiply the digits, they equal the same
   c) it is a multiple of 2   _____

8. a) each of the three digits is a different odd number
   b) it is a multiple of each of its digits
   c) it is less than 150   _____

Name _____

Let's Go on a Journey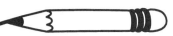

In each of the following books, the main character goes on a journey and most often learns some valuable lessons along the way. Travel with one of these characters as you read, then answer the questions.

The Hobbit by J. R. R. Tolkien
The Incredible Journey by Sheila Burnford
The High Voyage by Olga Litowinksy
Twenty-One Balloons by William Pene du Bois
A Door in the Wall by Marguerite de Angeli
Voyages of Doctor Dolittle by Hugh Lofting
North to Freedom by Anne Holm

Treasure Island by Robert Louis Stevenson
Phantom Tollbooth by Norton Juster
Adam of the Road by Elizabeth Gray
Walk Two Moons by Sharon Creech
The Night Journey by Katheryn Lasky
Homecoming by Cynthia Voigt

1. Title _____ Author _____

2. This journey was from _____
   to _____.

3. Describe one adventure on this journey.

   _____
   _____
   _____

4. What do you think the character learned as a result of that adventure?

   _____
   _____

5. Draw a map of the journey on the back of this paper.

6. If you could choose anywhere to go on a journey, where would you go? _____

   _____
   How would you get there? _____
   Who would go with you? _____
   What would you need to do to prepare for this journey? _____
   _____

Name _____

Man's Best Friend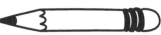

Animals have always intrigued people. We have tried to tame and make friends of all kinds, but some will always remain wild, free spirits. Many authors have tried to capture this relationship between people and animals. Choose one of the following books to read and then answer the questions.

Where the Red Fern Grows by Wilson Rawls   **The Incredible Journey** by Sheila Burnford
Summer of the Monkeys by Wilson Rawls   **Midnight Fox** by Betsy Byars
Old Yeller by Fred Gipson   Jim Kjelgaard books
Never Cry Wolf by Farlwy Mowat   **Black Stallion** by Walter Farley
Misty of Chincoteague by Marguerite Henry   **Cages** by Peg Kehret
King of the Wind by Marguerite Henry

1. Title _____ Author _____

2. Draw or describe the main animal(s) in the story.

   _____

3. What was something incredible this animal did? Is it realistic? Why or why not?

   _____

   _____

4. Many of these books have been made into movies. If you can, watch the movie. Compare the book to the movie. Write some of the differences in the columns below.

   Book   Movie

5. How would you describe the relationship between the animal and a person in the story? _____

6. If you could have an adventure with an animal of your choice, what would the animal be and what kind of adventure would you have? _____

   _____

   _____

Name _____

Out of This World

Each of the following books takes you to a fantasy world where you will encounter a whole new way of life and go on adventures you never dreamed of. Choose one of the books from the list and then complete the activities below.

The Giver by Lois Lowry
Tuck Everlasting by Natalie Babbit
The Hobbit by J.R.R. Tolkien
One of the Narnia Chronicles by C.S. Lewis
The Hero and the Crown by Robin McKinley
Grey King by Susan Cooper
The High King by Lloyd Alexander
A Wrinkle in Time by Madeleine L'Engle
Twenty-One Balloons by William Penne DuBois
Dinotopia by James Gurney
The Borrowers by Mary Norton
Redwall by Brian Jacques
Phantom Tollbooth by Norton Juster

1. Draw a picture on the back of this sheet of how you see the fantasy world in the book you chose.

2. Describe a typical day in the world (If none of the days were typical, pick one day you liked and tell about it)._____

_____

3. What did you like about this fantasy world? _____

4. What did you not like about it? _____

5. Describe the main character. _____

_____

6. If you could design your own fantasy world, what would it be like? Draw or describe it.

_____

_____

Name _____

Who Done It?

Each of the books listed below is a mystery. Join in the fun of searching for clues and figuring out "Who Done It?" Choose one of the following books to read. Then answer the questions below.

Encyclopedia Brown by Donald Sobol
Young Unicorns by Madeleine L'Engle
Who Really Killed Cock Robin by Jean George
Basil of Baker Street by Eve Titus
Dollhouse Murders by Betty Ren Wright
Wolves of Willoughby Chase by Joan Aiken
Egypt Game by Zilpha Keatley Snyder
Who Stole the Wizard of Oz? by Avi
Nancy Drew—Carolyn Keene—Hardy Boys by Franklin Dixon
Westing Game by Raskin Ellen
The View From the Cherry Tree by Willo Davis Roberts
The Tales of Sherlock Holmes by Arthur Conan Doyle

1. Title _____ Author _____

2. What is the mystery? _____

3. Describe the people or persons trying to solve the mystery.

   _____

   _____

4. What are some of the clues that helped to solve the mystery?

   _____

   _____

5. Who or what was the culprit?

   _____

6. What do you think was the culprit's biggest mistake? Why?

   _____

   _____

Name _____

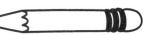

Survival!

Have you ever been stranded in a place where you had to depend on your own ingenuity to survive? Each of the following books is a story of survival, some in the wilderness, some in the midst of other people. Read one and experience with the characters the terror of finding yourself alone in a difficult situation, the struggle to weather the storm, and the triumph in persevering. Then answer the questions.

Hatchet, River, Canyons, The Voyage of the Frog by Gary Paulsen
The Cay by Theodore Taylor
Julie of the Wolves by Jean Craighead George
Swiss Family Robinson by Johann Wyss
Island of the Blue Dolphins by Scott O'Dell
The Diary of Ann Frank by Ann Frank
Journey to Topaz by Yoshiko Uchida
Snowbound by Harry Mazer
The Iceberg Hermit by Arthur Roth
Lost at Sea by Kate William
The Hiding Place by Corrie Ten Boom

1. Title _____ Author _____

2. Draw on the back of this sheet or describe below the place where the main character had to learn to survive.

   _____

   _____

3. How did the character get into this situation? _____

   _____

4. What are some of the survival skills the main character learned? _____

   _____

5. Was the character rescued? _____ If so, how did the character feel about being rescued? _____

   _____

6. If you were caught in this or a similar situation, what would you have done differently? _____

7. Which of the survival skills learned in this experience would help the character in his/her everyday life back at home? _____

Name _____

One Time in Our History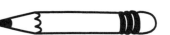

The following books are about people your age growing up during a particular time period in American history. Choose one book to read and find out what it was like to live back then, and then complete the activities on the bottom of the page.

Sarah, Plain and Tall by Patricia MacLachlan
Johnny Tremain by Esther Forbes
Roll of Thunder, Hear My Cry by Mildred D. Taylor
My Brother Sam Is Dead by James Lincoln Collier
Sign of the Beaver by Elizabeth George Speare
The Witch of Blackbird Pond by Elizabeth George Speare

Across Five Aprils by Irene Hunt
Journey to Topaz by Yoshiko Uchida
Sounder by William H. Armstrong
Caddie Woodlawn by Carol Brink
Roller Skates by Ruth Sawyer
I Am Regina by Sally Keehn

1. What is the title of the book you read? _____
   Who is the author? _____
   Give a brief summary of the book. _____
   _____
   _____

2. When and where does this story take place? _____

3. What did you like about life in this time period? _____
   _____

4. What was difficult about life then? _____
   _____

5. Sometimes, when you read a book, you feel like the characters are your friends. On the back of this page, write a letter to one of the characters. Respond to events in his/her life and tell about your life.

6. If you could travel back in time and give a character in the story one piece of advice or one invention that we have today, what would it be? Why?
   _____
   _____
   _____

Name _____

Another Place, Another Time

Each of the following stories takes place in a different country, culture, or period of history. Choose one to read and then answer the following questions.

Number the Stars by Lois Lowry
Morning Girl by Michael Dorris
Island of the Blue Dolphins by Scott O'Dell
The Bronze Bow by Elizabeth George Speare
White Stag by Kate Seredy
Young Fu of the Upper Yangtzee by Elizabeth Lewis
Catherine Called Birdie and **The Midwife's Apprentice** by Karen Cushman
The Pearl by John Steinbeck
A Door in the Wall by Marguerite de Angeli
Of Nightingales that Weep and **Sign of the Chrysanthemum** by Katherine Paterson
Secret of the Andes by Ann Clark
And Now, Miguel? by Joseph Krumgold
Gay Neck by Dhan Mukerji

1. Title _____ Author _____

2. When and where did the story take place? _____

3. What did you learn about customs of the culture?
   Food? Clothing? School? Holidays or celebrations? Houses? Families?

   _____

   _____

4. Which one of the characters would most likely be your friend if you lived then?
   _____ Why? _____

5. If you could join the characters in the story on one adventure or one day, what would
   it be? Describe that part of the story. _____

   _____

6. If you could ask the author one question about this book, what would it be?

   _____

   _____

Name _____

Growing Up Is Hard to Do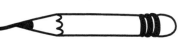

What are some of the struggles you face as you grow from childhood into adulthood? Maybe you can identify with characters in these stories who may be having similar struggles. Each of the following stories is about a young person close to your age. Choose one to read and answer the questions that follow.

Maniac Magee by Jerry Spinelli
Egypt Game by Zilpha Keatley Snyder
Shiloh by Phyllis Reynolds Naylor
Philip Hall Likes Me, I Reckon Maybe by Bette Greene
M C Higgins by Virginia Hamilton
Harriet the Spy by Louise Fitzhugh
Summer of the Swans by Betsy Byars
From the Mixed Up Files of Mrs. Basil E. Frankweiler and **The View from Saturday** by
    E. L. Konigsburg
Anastasia Krupnik by Lois Lowry
Where the Lilies Bloom by Vera Cleaver
Veronica Ganz by Nancy Robinson
Bridge to Terabithia by Katherine Paterson
Up a Road Slowly by Irene Hunt
Boys Start the War by Phyllis Reynolds Naylor
Walk Two Moons by Sharon Creech
The Homecoming and **Dicey's Song** by Cynthia Voigt

1. What is the title?_____ Author _____

2. What was the main conflict for the characters in this story?_____

3. How was it resolved? _____

4. What is one good choice or decision made by a character is this story?

    _____

5. If you were in the main character's place, what is one choice you might have made differently than he/she did in the story? _____

6. How would your choice have changed the story? Rewrite that part of the story to show how it would be different. (Use the back of this sheet.)

7. Draw a new cover design for the jacket of this book.

Name _____

Raffle a Book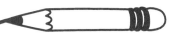

For a new twist on an oral book report, why not try raffling the privilege of being the next to borrow a great book?

After you read the book, prepare to raffle it by doing the following. Then follow the same order for giving the report.

1. Give some basic background information:

   Title: _____

   Author: _____

   Where it takes place: _____

   When it takes place: _____

   Other: _____

2. Choose an exciting passage from the book, between one and two pages long. Read it aloud using a lot of voice expression. Stop at an exciting part, so that people will want to find out what happens next. page _____

3. Ask a question that requires a very specific response based on the background information or what you read. Anyone who knows the answer should write it on a small scrap of paper along with their name.

   Question: _____

   Answer: _____

4. For those who answered correctly, place their papers in a bag. Shake the bag and draw out a name. That person is the lucky winner to be the next one to read the book and find out what happened when you stopped reading.

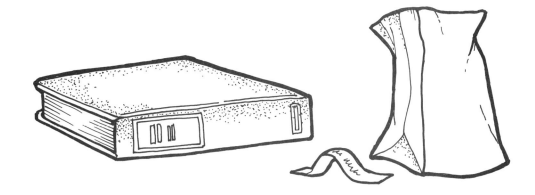

Name _____

Book Charades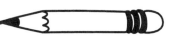

This game can be played in teams or with an entire class together. Cut out the book title cards and put them in a box, bag, or other container. Select one student to go first (or if using teams, one student per team). Draw a card out of the bag. Students must act out the book title, not a scene from the book. If playing with the whole class, the first person to guess the whole title is the next player to act. If playing with teams, the first team to guess the title wins a point. Variations: 1. Draw the title instead of acting. 2. Wrap the title cards around a gummy worm. The person who guesses the title first gets to eat the "book worm."

Little House on the Prairie

My Side of the Mountain

The Lion, the Witch and the Wardrobe

Walk Two Moons

The Plant Who Ate Dirty Socks

Indian in the Cupboard

Roll of Thunder, Hear My Cry

Catherine Called Birdy

A Wrinkle in Time

The Hero and the Crown

Sign of the Beaver

Call It Courage

Where the Red Fern Grows

Island of the Blue Dolphins

The View from Saturday

Sarah, Plain and Tall

The Adventures of Huckleberry Finn

Treasure Island

Number the Stars

King of the Wind

Egypt Game

Slave Dancer

Summer of the Swans

Up a Road Slowly

Name _____

Authors

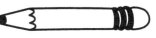

Find the names of twenty-nine authors in the word search puzzle. Besides the obvious fact that they all wrote books, what do all of these authors have in common?

```
J O K A T H E R I N E P A T E R S O N N E L L
E E D C V U W A R D T O C R R B R E T R L P S
R X A Y M I L D R E D T A Y L O R N A O G P E
R C Y N T H I A R Y L A N T R E B E Y P N A R
Y Y H G C K M E I W R O L Z S T P D S H E T H
S N I M E R R D S K J U I B T S A C A V L R J
P T R A P T A S C O T T O D E L L Y N R E I T
I H W E N M S I A R O C K G E C A T Y O N C N
N I M G D E L N G W U T R X D U C K R L I I K
E A H A T I W H E H R O A W H E R E A Y E A R
L V O E S B A C I R E N E H U N T M E A L M E
L O I S L O W R Y G D A C A P H U T L N E A L
I I M O F O X Y H E P P D B A P H E C S D C R
G G S O H C N T R S O S A G K A T E Y D A L O
T H E R E G E W R R S S P P E M O C L L M A B
E T H U B B D E E J O A K O N O J U R O E C I
F U N Y A T Y Y S R O L L I N G R T E N A H N
L E E Z M B W I R I S P R D R E P G V Y A L M
S N I F Y A M P U L M D E F F O P L E E W A C
E L P S S K A T H D Y U P C A R O L B R I N K
E S T H E R F O R B E S O P L A I D S S G H I
S E T N U T R P M I N X O F A L U A P I C C N
B U T T O N O P C W N V C U S C M W A L E L L
R E F T X I W I N E S P N S I L L Y P Y M B E
S R G N O R T S M R A M A I L L I W E H P O Y
Q U E D O E L K O N I G S B U R G M E P H I L
N A N E T S C Y M A R G U E R I T E H E N R Y
P A U X P A U L F L E I S C H M A N H A T E N
```

Name _____

Scavenger Hunt

Shanda and Bob went on a bike ride one Saturday afternoon. They read all these different signs, posters, bumper stickers, and advertisements along the way.

HONK if you love Elvis!

Terrace Boulevard

COME SEE ♪ The ♪ Music ♪ Man August 11-15

STU'S SHOES Our penny loafers ain't cheap

TRY OUR MOUTH-WATERING AVOCADO MAYONNAISE

Dr. Nipsy Tastes smooth, less filling... ONLY 5 CALORIES PER BOTTLE

YIELD RIGHT OF WAY

Mary Tsoski for School Board

SHOW PRIDE ☆☆☆☆☆☆ BUY AMERICAN

SPEED 30 M.P.H. LIMIT

5TH FEDERAL BANK YES, WE CARE

Kaline Ball Park 2 blocks

Use the signs to answer the following questions.

1. What was the speed limit? _____

2. What was the name of the ball park? _____

3. What is "less filling"? _____

4. What street did they find? _____

5. What flavor of mayonnaise was advertised? _____

6. When was **The Music Man** showing? _____

7. Who is Mary Tsoski? _____

8. What "ain't cheap"? _____

9. When should you honk? _____

10. What is the fifth? _____

Name _____

Folklore Newspaper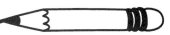

As you read each news article, think about the main idea.

1. It was a great shock to me. You know, the story of Rapunzel who was nabbed by an evil witch. Do you remember her long hair? Well, hold your britches. The scoop is that it really wasn't her own hair. No siree! It seems she and the witchy-poo had a wig business going for nigh unto five years. I always wondered how anyone could grow hair as long as that.

2. Don't tell me you believed that story about the wicked wolf blowing down the houses of two of the three little pigs? That's hogwash. I mean, have you ever tried blowing down even a one-foot pile of sticks? Hard to imagine. Now **Folklore Newspaper** has heard from reliable but anonymous sources that the wolf purchased seven powerful electric fans. That is the only reasonable solution short of a tornado. Seriously.

3. Ever hear of Mattie Habler? Probably not. Over time, people have given her the handle Mother Hubbard. Why? Well, we don't know. We can only imagine it's because Hubbard rhymes with cupboard. After all, Mattie was no one's mother. Shoot! She was a mean-spirited, hateful hag, and she was finally kicked out of Gooseberg when she starved that poor dog. No one has heard from her since. And there's no truth to her lookin' in her cupboard for dog biscuits or puppy food with the poor pooch pawing at her feet. The dog, a long, thin St. Bernard, was kept chained in a minuscule pen in her backyard. No love lost between those two, let me tell ya.

4. Bob Horner's kid, Jack, was one mischievous little rascal. Ol' Bob never knew quite what to do with that boy. Seems whenever I'd go over for a game of checkers, the boy would either be confined in his room for some transgression, or he'd be sittin' in the kitchen corner. That Jack! He had this wonderful grin and the prettiest twinkle in his eyes. Bob could never stay angry with him for long. One time the nervy kid dipped his thumb into a freshly baked cherry pie (no plums at Christmas for him) right in front of his pa. Then he smiled and said, "I'm a good boy, I am, huh, da?" Old Bob just rolled his eyes and shook his head.

Write an appropriate headline for each story from the **Folklore Newspaper**. The attention-grabbing headline should fit the tone and main idea of the story.

1. _____

   _____

2. _____

   _____

3. _____

   _____

4. _____

   _____

Name _____

Reading in the Content Areas

Use this with any reading assignment.

1. Before you read, write down what you already know about this topic.

_____

_____

_____

2. What are some questions you would like answered as you read?

_____

_____

_____

_____

3. Read the assignment.

4. What did you learn?

_____

_____

_____

_____

_____

5. Do you still have questions that were not answered? _____
   Where can you find these answers?

_____

_____

_____

world map

Where in the World?

Label the following on the world map.

Equator   Prime Meridian   Asia   Antarctica   Arctic Ocean
Arctic Circle   Antarctic Circle   Europe   Pacific Ocean   Atlantic Ocean
North America   South America   Africa   Indian Ocean   Australia

Tropic of Cancer
Tropic of Capricorn
International Date Line

Name _____

IF8679 A Little Bit of Everything

Name _____

Map Review

Use the clues to fill in the crossword puzzle.

Across

1. maps that show how such things as population, rainfall, language, etc. are distributed.
4. a model of the earth
5. A _____ on a map shows direction.
7. The prime meridian divides the earth into east and west _____.
11. Lines of ____ run east and west parallel to each other north and south of the equator.
14. a map maker
16. another name for lines of longitude
17. The _____ divides the earth into north and south hemispheres.
18. a map that shows mountains, rivers, and other natural features
19. maps that show information from the past

Down

2. A _____ tells you what the distance on the map is compared to actual distance.
3. imaginary lines running north and south through the North and South Poles
6. the first letters of the cardinal directions
8. a flat representation of the earth or any part of it
9. a map that shows countries, cities, states
10. a map that shows the height of the land above sea level
12. seven major land forms on earth
13. The _____ tells what each symbol stands for on a map.
15. another name for lines of latitude

Name _____

Out of Africa

Label the following on the physical map of Africa

Mt. Kilimanjaro	Zambezi River	Atlas Mountains	Sahara Desert
Nile River	Kalahari Desert	Mediterranean Sea	Great Rift Valley
Sahel	Red Sea	Niger River	Lake Victoria

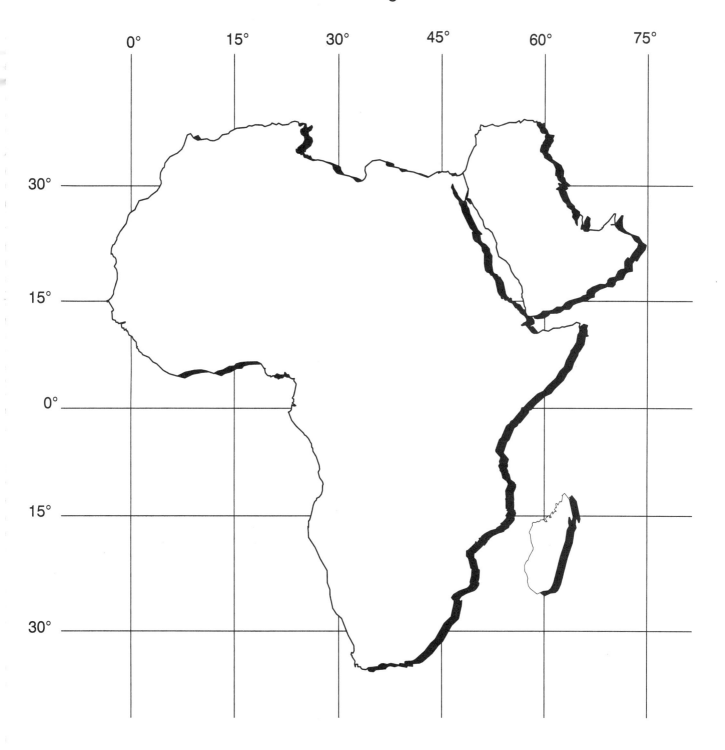

Name _____

African Scavenger Hunt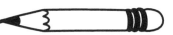

Use an atlas to conduct a scavenger hunt across Africa. As you travel, identify the absolute location for each of these natural features.

1. Mt. Kilimanjaro is Africa's highest point. It is located at _____°S_____°E.
2. Next you go to Djibouti and Africa's lowest point, Lake Assal, at _____.
3. Then it is on to Africa's largest country, Sudan, and its capital, Khartoum, at _____.
4. Cairo, Egypt, is Africa's largest metropolitan area, located at _____.
5. Then head to Lagos, Nigeria, the second largest metropolitan area, at _____.
6. Next, go to the third largest metro area of Kinshasa, Zaire, at _____.
7. Traveling Africa's longest river, the Nile, takes you through Lake Nasser at_____.
8. Africa's second longest river is the Zaire/Congo at _____.
9. The Niger River is Africa's third longest at _____.
10. In Africa you will find the world's largest desert, the Sahara, at _____.
11. Another of Africa's deserts is the Kalahari, where you meet the San people at _____.
12. You travel the unique coastal Namib Desert at _____.
13. Head to Africa's largest lake, Victoria, at _____.
14. Then you see the second largest lake, Tanganyika, at _____.
15. Next you head to the Cape of Good Hope at _____.
16. Africa's truly southern point is Cape Agulhas at _____.
17. Stop by Victoria Falls at _____ on the Zambezi River.
18. Travel into the Great Rift Valley at _____.
19. Here you visit the Olduvai Gorge, where humans first walked this continent, at_____.
20. Next, visit Timbuktu, known for its gold, salt, and slave trading at _____.
21. Walvis Bay is your next stop, and it is not a body of water, at _____.
22. Cabinda comes next at _____, with its rich oil fields for Angola.
23. And you finish at the Great Karroo Plateau at _____.

You have now found and visited many of the outstanding locations of Africa. Hope you enjoyed your travels!

Design your own scavenger hunt, maze, or board game using some of Africa's absolute locations. Consider making your outline pattern based on African facts you have learned.

Name _____

Relative Location in Africa

Africa is a huge, plateau continent with about one fifth of the earth's land surface. It is positioned across the equator, creating variable precipitation and low-fertility soils that cause environmental problems for farming and population distribution. Rich in raw materials and with less than one tenth of the world's population, Africa has great potential.

Listed below are the ten most populous cities in Africa. Locate each on the map.

Cairo, Egypt   Abidjan, Cote D'Ivoire
Lagos, Nigeria   Cape Town, South Africa
Kinshasa, Zaire   Dakar, Senegal
Casablanca, Morocco   Addis Ababa, Ethiopia
Alexandria, Egypt   Algiers, Algeria

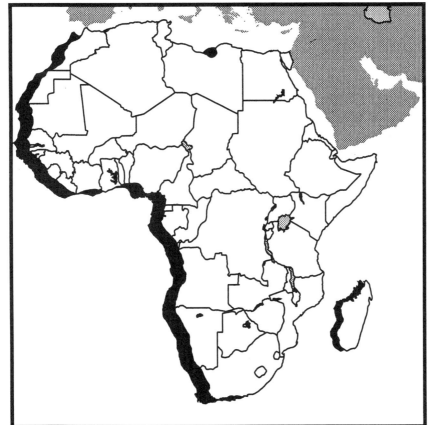

Answer the following questions. As you do, you will be using relative location, that is, using descriptive words and phrases to identify a place. Use the back of this page if you need more room.

1. Describe where the most populous African cities are located. _____

2. Which country or region contains the most cities? _____

3. Are the majority in coastal or inland locations? _____

4. Are any of these cities the capitals of their country? _____

5. Why would so many Africans choose to live in these cities? _____

Name _____

Coming to America

Label the following on the maps of the Americas.

Great Lakes	Rocky Mountains	Amazon River	Mt. McKinley
Hudson Bay	Andes Mountains	Colorado River	Patagonia
Tiera del Fuego	Gulf of Mexico	Appalachian Mts.	Rio Grande
Caribbean Sea	Gulf of St. Lawrence	Yucatán Peninsula	Bering Strait
Strait of Magellan	Mississippi River	Isthmus of Panama	Lake Titicaca

Color the map.

Name _____

North American Scramble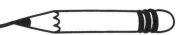

Here are some scrambled locations in North America. See if you can unscramble the letters, using the clue "This is in North America . . . ."

M C I X O E   1. It is not Canada or the United States

S R P O U E I R   2. It is the world's second largest as well as the highest and deepest of the five.

G A N E D R E N L   3. It is really a "bowl filled with ice" that belongs with Europe.

B O D A S R A B   4. It is the easternmost Caribbean island.

N A R A I G A   5. You do not have to tumble over it in a barrel.

M E N C L I Y K   6. It soars above like its Indian name—Denali, which means "high one."

W E E A A A L L I   7. It is located on the Pacific-drenched windward side of Kauai.

B U D E M A R   8. Its coral beaches belong with Europe.

B S M H A A A   9. Columbus first landed here in the Atlantic, finding no rivers and not finding "India."

P M N A A A   10. It is a link between oceans and continents.

C D N A A A   11. It is known for its size, its two official languages, its north magnetic pole, and its open border.

A L S I N E T L   12. There is a Greater and a Lesser.

D A H E T   Y L E A L V   13. It is no wonder it is the lowest place in this region.

S U Q A O I E   14. It is the biggest plant California has to offer.

C U B O M A L I   15. It crosses from its source in Canada to join the Snake in the United States.

A A E I U L N T   16. These islands are so far west you might think they belong with Russia in Asia.

U E T N I D   E T S A T S   17. It is the most populous country in this region.

R O I   E R D A G N   18. It divides English- and Spanish-speaking people.

R Y C K O   19. These rugged mountains span from Canada into the United States.

R O D O W E D   20. These grand and lanky California trees add color to their timber.

Name _____

Climograph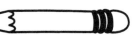

Design a climograph, using the following temperature and precipitation data.

	Jan.	Feb.	Mar.	April	May	June	July	Aug.	Sept.	Oct.	Nov.	Dec.
Temp.	37.2	38.3	44.1	54.3	61.5	68.9	75.0	77.7	71.6	60.6	50.4	41.4
Precip.	2.0	2.6	4.3	5.3	5.9	6.3	5.6	4.6	7.5	7.2	4.3	2.3

1. Does this climate have a wet or dry winter? _____

2. Does this climate have a wet or dry summer? _____

3. Does this climate's warmest month average above 71.6°F?

   _____

4. Does this climate's coolest month average below 41.4°F?

   _____

5. Does this climate have at least one month below 32°F? _____

6. Does this climate have all months averaging above 32°F? _____

7. Does this place seem to be north or south of the equator? _____

8. Does this place appear to be near the equator? _____

9. Does this place seem to be close to an ocean? _____

10. Does this place appear to be near mountains? _____

11. This place is a humid subtropical climate type. Using an atlas, name some places in North America that have this type of climate. _____

_____

_____

Write a descriptive paragraph about this place. Use the climate factors from the data and climograph. Would you want to live in this place? Why or why not?

_____

_____

_____

_____

All Around Asia

Name _____

Label the following on the physical map of Asia.

Himalayas	Indochina Peninsula	Euphrates River	Siberia	Arabian Sea	Huang He River
Mt. Everest	Ganges River	Tigres River	Gobi Desert	Sea of Japan	Plateau of Tibet

IF8679 A Little Bit of Everything

Name _____

Asia ————————————————————————

With the vastness of Asia, we can best see this location from above the earth. Let's take a trip by air to pinpoint many of these places you have read about. We will begin in Southeast Asia and travel clockwise around this region. Get your passport, an atlas, and we're off from western North America . . . to Java (most densely populated area of the world) in Indonesia at 1._____°S _____°E, on to Singapore at 2._____°N _____°E for some shopping at Lucky Plaza, then to 3._____°N _____°E to visit in the capital, Bandar Seri Begawan, built on stilts in one of the world's wealthiest nations.

Leaving Brunei, we go over former French Indochina and the Mekong River to Cambodia (or Kampuchea) and Tonle Sap at 4._____°N _____°E, which can quadruple in size during the monsoon season.

Monsoons also affect Bangladesh, so we're off to Dhaka on the delta of the Ganges-Brahmaputra Rivers at 5._____°N _____°E to visit houses on mud platforms.

Our next lofty destination is high in the Himalayas of Nepal (on the border with China)—Mt. Everest at 6._____°N _____°E—we're on top of the world at 29,864 feet. Next we come back down to earth with millions of people in Bombay, India, at 7._____°N _____°E, purchasing some textiles, maybe a colorful sari or a homespun dhoti.

Next we'll slip over the Khyber Pass, as invaders often did heading into Southwest Asia at 8._____°N _____°E, before making our way to 9._____°N _____°E and the Sinai Peninsula, also seeing the Suez Canal.

From this northeast corner of Egypt we travel to the Dead Sea at 10._____°N _____°E to prove we can truly float in this salty water; then it's on to Istanbul, Turkey—also known historically as Constantinople—(the only city in the world on two continents) at 11._____°N _____°E.

The next leg of this journey finds us passing over the boundary line many mapmakers use to divide Asia from Europe with the Caspian Sea at 12._____°N _____°E, and into the treeless tundra of Russia's Arctic north to Franz Josef Land above the Arctic Circle—and Asia's northern edge—at 13._____°N _____°E—brrrrrrrr, cold!

Flying in a great circle route southeast to 14._____°N _____°E, we arrive in the world's largest city, Tokyo, Japan . . . how about some Disney fun while we're here before we head to 15._____°N _____°E for some kimchi in Seoul, South Korea?

Manchuria's (or as the Chinese prefer "Northeast") coal and oil fields can be seen at 16._____°N _____°E around Harbin as we fly over, going southwest past the Great Wall of China to see the capital, Beijing, at 17._____°N _____°E, then further along China's Grand Canal route to 18._____°N _____°E and Shanghai, the world's largest city.

We finish our Asian travels in Hong Kong at 19._____°N _____°E, fascinated by the modern skyscrapers.

Create a paragraph about your personal impressions of your trip.

Name _____

What Is My Name?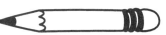

For this assignment, you are to become a geographical specialist to identify these Asian locations. Use your analytical abilities and any reference material you need to reveal the identity of each of these Asian features. Some are real world champions!

1. I am the largest saltwater lake in the world. I am surrounded by five nations, and my surface is 92 feet below sea level. I have a depression on my northern shoreline, and it is no wonder my mental state leaves me with an identity crisis, because everyone calls me a sea—I'm so depressed! ____

2. I am the world's largest sea. My name is tied to Southeast and East Asia, but cousin East has his own identity . . . don't ask me what happened to cousins North and West. I create a split personality for Malaysia. _____

3. I get two claims to fame! I am the lowest point on land and the lowest lake in the world. My surface water is 1,302 feet below sea level to be exact. I am so salty that I am uninhabitable and much saltier than the oceans. Wow! _____

4. I am the largest peninsula in the world. My shape like a snow boot is really misleading because my dry climate would not produce that kind of precipitation. My identity is shared with others in this region, a country, a culture, and a language. Sharing is wonderful! _____

5. I am the oldest and deepest lake in the world, but I still do not get the respect I deserve. Children slide on my icy surface in the parts that remain frozen for up to seven months of the year.

   _____

6. I am the largest bay in the world. The Andaman and Nicobar islands are located in me. Between the maze of channels across the world's largest delta from the Ganges-Brahmaputra rivers dumping water into me and my high tides during the summer monsoon, I feel like I barely keep my head above water! _____

7. I am the largest archipelago in the world. My 13,677 islands string together under the motto "unity in diversity." With some 300 ethnic groups speaking more than 250 languages, we crowd onto just a few of these many islands.

   _____

8. I am the color my name implies because algae live in my sea water. The sands of Egyptian and Arabian deserts also irritate my eyes, making them this color.

   _____

9. I am a Chinese river that they call Huang He. My "color" name comes from the tons of soil called loess I carry from the great Gobi Desert of interior Asia into a sea. This must be my sibling called by the same color-name. You might as well identify us both!

   _____ _____

10. I am Asia's longest estuary, and I am also one of the few rivers that flows into the Arctic Ocean. Does that make me a twin? Not necessarily, if you know what an estuary is. Mine is 550 miles long and as wide as 50 miles. _____

Name _____

Exploring Europe

Label the following on the physical map of Europe.

North Sea	Caspian Sea	English Channel	Baltic Sea
Seine River	Caucasus Mountains	Adriatic Sea	Danube River
Ural Mountains	Mediterranean Sea	Apennines	Iberian Peninsula
Bay of Biscay	Pyrenees	Scandinavian Peninsula	

Name _____

Absolute Location in Europe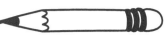

Using an atlas, give the absolute location of:
1. London, England   _____
2. Rome, Italy   _____
3. Helsinki, Finland   _____

4. Moscow, Russia   _____
5. Oral, Kazakhstan   _____
6. your town   _____

If it is 10:00 P.M. in Greenwich, England, what time is it in
7. Helsinki, Finland?   _____

8. Oral, Kazakhstan? _____

Using an atlas, give the absolute location of:
9. Reykjavík, Iceland   _____
10. Dublin, Ireland   _____

11. Lisbon, Portugal   _____
12. Madrid, Spain   _____

If it is 5:00 A.M. in Greenwich, England, what time is it in
13. Reykjavík, Iceland? _____

14. Madrid, Spain?   _____

15. Looking at a globe, if it is Wednesday in Europe and you are traveling from Athens, Greece, what day of the week is it in Washington, D.C., when you fly across the Atlantic Ocean? _____

16. Still using the globe, your flight leaves Washington, D.C., and you have a layover in San Francisco, California. What happens to the day of the week?_____

17. After getting on your San Francisco flight, you travel across the Pacific Ocean, landing in Tokyo, Japan. What day of the week is it?   _____

18. You leave Athens, Greece, at 2:00 P.M. on Wednesday and land in Washington, D.C., seven time zones earlier. How is this possible? _____

_____

19. You leave San Francisco at 4:00 A.M. on Thursday and land in Japan on Wednesday. How is this possible?_____

_____

20. By measuring with a globe and a piece of string, answer the following question: Is it shorter to travel from Athens, Greece, to Tokyo, Japan, flying across the Atlantic Ocean, the United States, and the Pacific Ocean or from Athens, Greece, to Tokyo, Japan, flying in a great-circle route?   _____

_____

21. Why is it important to know how to use a time zone map? _____

_____

22. Why is it important for airplanes to fly using great-circle routes? _____

_____

Name _____

Relative Location in Europe ~~~~~~~~~~~~~ ⊃≡ ﹚﹚

Using an atlas, give the relative location of each of these places in Europe:

1. Oslo, Norway, is located on the _____ Peninsula. It is on the Skagerrak side of the _____ Sea.

2. Copenhagen, Denmark, is on the _____ Peninsula on the _____ Sea side of Scandinavia.

3. Barcelona, Spain, was the site of the 1992 Summer Olympic Games. Barcelona is also a major industrial port on the_____Sea near the _____ Mountains on the _____ Peninsula.

4. Sicily is the southern island off the tip of the _____ Peninsula in the _____ Sea. Sardinia is the western Italian island separated from Italy by the _____ Sea.

5. San Marino is an independent republic surrounded by the country of _____. This nation also surrounds the State of the Vatican City, which is located in the capital, _____.

6. The Peloponnesus is a southern peninsula on the _____ Peninsula as part of Greece. The _____ Sea is on Greece's western side and the _____ Sea is on its eastern side.

7. Crete is an island off the _____ coast of Greece. It is separated from Greece by the Sea of _____.

8. Circle the European nations from each group that are landlocked:

Poland	Switzerland	Russia	Croatia
Hungary	France	Ukraine	Bosnia
Romania	Belgium	Latvia	Macedonia
Bulgaria	Netherlands	Moldova	Albania

9. The Sierra Nevada mountain range is located on the southern Iberian Peninsula in _____ on the _____ Sea.

10. The Scottish Highlands are on the _____ Isles in the political unit of _____.

11. Ireland and _____ are separated from the other parts of the United Kingdom (British Isles) by the _____ Sea.

12. The _____ Mountains divide Russia into a European and an Asian section. Kazakhstan, Georgia, Azerbaijan, and Turkey are also divided between _____ and Asia. The _____ Sea borders Kazakhstan, Russia, and Azerbaijan. The _____ Sea borders Turkey, Russia, Ukraine, Romania, and Bulgaria.

S.W.O.T. Team

We're forming a S.W.O.T. team to assess strengths (S), weaknesses (W), opportunities (O), and threats (T) in Europe's environment. Use the following to assess each scenario and circle your choices. Be prepared to defend them.

Strength (S): a positive act being done to protect or preserve the environment

Weakness (W): a negative thing that is harmful or destructive to the environment

Opportunity (O): a hopeful chance to change or improve the environment

Threat (T): a warning that predicts the possibility of damage done to the environment

S W O T   1. Factories belch chemical-laden smoke.

S W O T   2. Geothermal energy in use.

S W O T   3. Burning lignite, or brown coal, produces sulfur dioxide emissions.

S W O T   4. Oil spill off the Shetland Islands in the North Sea.

S W O T   5. Use of unleaded gasoline in cars and trucks.

S W O T   6. Stiffening security requirements in chemical industries.

S W O T   7. Listing sites and contents at nuclear waste sites.

S W O T   8. Nine out of ten children in some cities suffer from respiratory tract problems.

S W O T   9. Ban on hunting minke whales.

S W O T   10. Establishing "quiet zones" to prevent low-flying aircraft and snow-mobiles in nature preserves

S W O T   11. Governments buying back farmlands to convert to natural habitats.

S W O T   12. Use of bottled water.

S W O T   13. Placing taxes on energy and carbon dioxide emissions.

S W O T   14. Creating a multi-national park along floodplain areas.

S W O T   15. Use of natural gas instead of coal and oil.

S W O T   16. Rise in the number of endangered species.

S W O T   17. Runoff of animal manures and fertilizers from farmlands.

S W O T   18. Pollution monitoring stations placed in some areas.

S W O T   19. Thyroid tumors in children are the first proof of cancer resulting from Chernobyl nuclear reactor explosion.

Name _____

Relative Location in the CIS

The CIS (Commonwealth of Independent States) extends almost halfway around the world. When the sun rises over Ukraine, it is setting over eastern Siberia. The longest coastline in the world is in the Commonwealth. This entire region is north of 35°N latitude. The chart below gives the land area (in square miles) and the size rank in the world for each of the 11 countries included in the Commonwealth of Independent States (CIS).

Country	Area (square miles)	Global Rank
Armenia	11,500	133
Azerbaijan	33,400	111
Belarus	80,200	84
Kazakhstan	1,049,200	9
Kyrgyzstan	75,642	85
Moldova	13,012	130
Russia	6,592,800	1
Tajikistan	55,300	93
Turkmenistan	188,417	51
Ukraine	233,100	43
Uzbekistan	172,700	55

Using an atlas and the information above, answer the following questions.

1. Which is the smallest of the nations in the CIS? _____

2. If European Russia is approximately 1,747,112 square miles, how much area does Asian Russia cover? _____

3. Which countries in the Commonwealth are among the world's ten largest? _____

4. Which CIS nation is closest to the Tropic of Cancer? _____

5. Which Commonwealth country is crossed by the Arctic Circle?_____

6. Which country in the Commonwealth is closest to the International Date Line? _____

7. Which countries in the CIS border the Caspian Sea, the lowest point in Europe?_____

   _____

   _____

8. Parts of Russia, Kazakhstan, Georgia, and Azerbaijan are European. Which CIS nations are completely Asian?_____

   _____

   _____

9. Mount Elbrus in Russia is the highest point in Europe at 18,510 feet above sea level. What mountain range contains this peak? _____

Name _____

Meet Me in the Middle East

Label the following on the physical map of the Middle East.

Mediterranean Sea	Jordan River	Syrian Desert	Caspian Sea
Black Sea	Dead Sea	Persian Gulf	Arabian Peninsula
Arabian Sea	Red Sea	Euphrates River	Tigris River

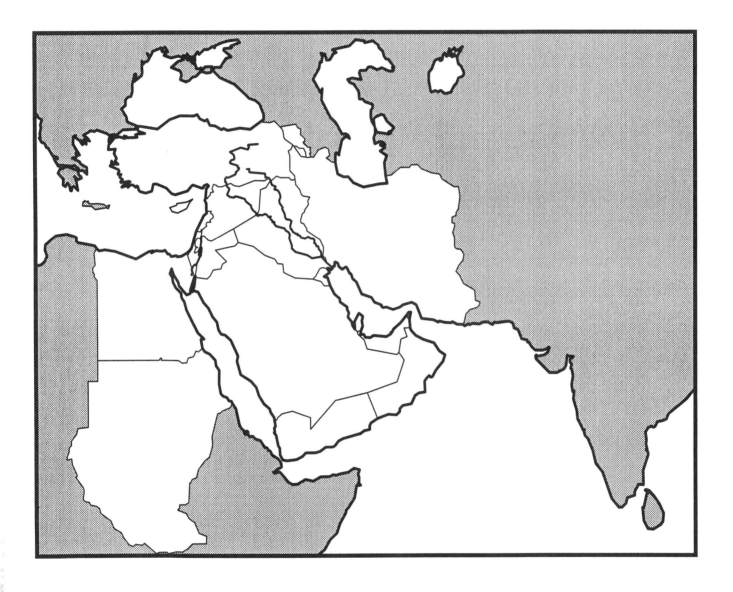

Name _____

Relative Location in North Africa/Middle East

The following relative location descriptions can be completed using an atlas.

1. This nation is largely Asian. It includes the Anatolia Plateau. The western peninsula contains Istanbul, the largest city (that once was Constantinople)—the only city in the world on two continents. The country is about twice the size of California and is European and Asian. The strategic locations of the straits, Bosporus and Dardanelles, as well as the Black Sea and Mediterranean Sea, give this nation many advantages. It is also the source for the Tigris and Euphrates Rivers. WHAT COUNTRY IS THIS? _____

2. The Sinai Peninsula is in this country. Through it, this country connects Africa and Asia. It also has the Suez Canal and Nile River to supply it with water and income. Parts of the Sahara— the Arabian, Libyan, and Nubian Deserts—cover much of its landscape. It is about the size of Texas, Oklahoma, and Arkansas combined.
   WHAT COUNTRY IS THIS? _____

3. Many describe this nation as the climate crossroads of the world. It has the Negev Desert, the Jordan River, the Dead Sea, and the Sea of Galilee, which create climate diversity. The flora and fauna found here represent those found in Europe, Asia, and Africa. This country is about the size of New Jersey.
   WHAT COUNTRY IS THIS? _____

4. Many call this nation's great desert the "Empty Quarter"; to Arabic speakers it is the Rub al Khali. This country is one third the size of the United States. The Red Sea and Persian Gulf form this country's western and eastern borders. It is the core of the peninsula that shares part of its name. WHAT IS THIS COUNTRY? _____

5. The smallest of the nations in this region encompasses 35 sand-covered islands located in the Persian Gulf. Only six of these islands are inhabited. Causeways link this island nation with two other islands and Saudi Arabia's mainland. It is smaller than New York City. WHAT IS THIS COUNTRY? _____

6. Africa is closest to Europe at this nation's northern tip. Spain is only nine miles across the Strait of Gibraltar. This nation is larger than California. It is known as the Far West in the Arab countries of northwest Africa called the Maghreb—which means "west." It also claims Western Sahara as part of its territory; however, a vote to settle the dispute over this claim has been prevented from taking place.
   WHAT COUNTRY IS THIS? _____

7. In the extreme eastern edge of this region is a nation about the size of Texas that is often studied with South Asia. The Khyber Pass, which became the link between Southwest and South Asia, caused this country to be called the "crossroads of Central Asia." A landlocked nation covered with mountains and desert, this nation has been invaded numerous times, resulting in ethnic and tribal diversity.
   WHAT IS THIS COUNTRY? _____

Name _____

Oceania

Read the following passage. Use the vocabulary words in bold to fill in the blanks below. Use the numbered letters to fill in the blanks at the bottom of the page.

The high islands of **Oceania** are mainly **volcanic mountain** peaks. **Rainfall** is adequate on these islands because the mountains catch the **winds**. With the rich **volcanic** soil and abundant moisture, plants and crops grow well. **Forest** landscapes provide building materials for boats and houses. Many high islands also have valuable mineral resources. Because of their larger size and varied resources, these islands can support greater human populations and provide a better standard of living for their people.

The low islands of Oceania are characterized as being mainly **coral reefs** or **atolls** surrounding **lagoons**. Coral polyps, tiny sea creatures, build reefs with their hard outer skeletons. An atoll is a reef built around a volcano by innumerable coral. Over time, the volcano wears away or sinks beneath the **water**, while the reef continues to grow. Finally, the reef breaks through the surface of the water, forming a ring-shaped atoll or chain of islets (very small islands). Because these islands are so hard-surfaced, the rainfall they receive often runs off. Many islands suffer **droughts** because they do not have the mountains to catch the moisture-laden winds. The little soil they have is thin and sandy and is often broken and washed away by wind and waves. Drinking water is often scarce. **Guano**, bird droppings used as phosphate fertilizer, is the most valuable low island resource besides **fishing** and some agricultural products such as root crops and fruits, mainly **coconut**. Widely scattered groups of people live on these islands, but they live mostly a **subsistence** existence. There are some commercial plantations producing coffee, pineapples, and sugar cane. **Flora** and **fauna** in Oceania are dependent on how far the island is from its Asian source. Isolated islands have no mammals except the bat, no amphibians or reptiles except the sea turtle, and hardly any land birds. Remoteness has also preserved some ancient species (black pearls, Australia's marsupials, and the bird of paradise).

C _ _ _ _ _
    1

F _ _ _ _
 2

_ _ _ _ A
 3

_ U _ _ _ _
4

_ _ _ F _
     5

_ _ I _ _
6

W _ _ _ _
   7

_ I _ _ _
  8

_ _ _ _ _ T
     9

_ _ _ _ _ U _
10   11

_ I _ _ _ _
   12

_ A _ _ _ _ _
13

_ _ _ A _ _ _
      14

_ _ O _ _ _ _
15   16

_ _ _ _ I _ _ _
      17

_ _ _ N _ _ _ _
18

_ _ _ L _ _ _ _ _
    19

_ _ _ S _ _ _ _ _ _
20   21

_ _ _ _ _   _ _ _ _ _ _ _ _ _   _ _ _   _ _ _ _ _ _ _ _
12 14 4 16   18 21 8 1 19 15 5   3 10 6   17 9 13 2 11 7 20

(145)

Name _____

World Records

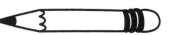

Listed below are 14 world records. Unscramble the words in the word box to find who holds each record.

TOUHS CRAAFI	LINE	DRANGLENE	TROHN CREAMIA
GANATAPIO	ZAMANO	SNEAD	YIMAAALHS
ADED ESA	SAAI	PISNAAC ASE	TERIFEL STRECENC
TRAGE LALW FO NACIH		ISAA	

1. _____ longest coastline of any continent

2. _____ more of the world's people than any other

3. _____ the world's longest mountain chain

4. _____ the world's longest river

5. _____ the world's largest gold deposits

6. _____ the largest inland body of water on earth

7. _____ the largest desert in the Americas

8. _____ the world's biggest island

9. _____ the highest mountains on earth

10. _____ the biggest man-made structure on earth

11. _____ the second longest river on earth

12. _____ the world's largest continent

13. _____ the lowest point on earth

14. _____ It is believed that the first people lived here.

Name _____

A River Runs Through It

Choose words from the word bank to match with each description of amazing facts about the Nile River.

Word Bank:
Pyramids	cubit	Aswan Dam	Delta
Osiris	Sirius	Rosetta Stone	White and Blue
4,000+ miles	Euphrates River		
Milky Way	cataracts		

1. _____ Egyptian Pharaoh called this river in Syria "the river that flows the wrong way"; as far as he was concerned, all rivers should flow from the south to the north as does the Nile.

2. _____ monuments built on the banks of the Nile River. The builders shipped materials down the river to build these monuments.

3. _____ an important discovery on the banks of the Nile River which helped archeologists to interpret Egyptian hieroglyphics

4. _____ length of the Nile River, longest in the world

5. _____ unit of measurement used to mark the levels of the flooding of the Nile. Twelve meant hunger, thirteen, sufficiency, fourteen, joy, fifteen, security, and sixteen, abundance.

6. _____ Egyptians based their calendar on the rising of this star which marked the beginning of the rising of the Nile.

7. _____ The Egyptians thought this was the Nile River stretching across the heavens.

8. _____ the god of the Nile

9. _____ fertile area at the mouth of the Nile River named because it had the same shape as the Greek letter of this name

10. _____ the two rivers that join together to make the mighty Nile

11. _____ There are six of these waterfalls along the Nile as it travels through Egypt.

12. _____ built to help control the flooding of the Nile River

Choose one of these amazing facts about the Nile River. Research and find out more about it. Share your research with your class.

Name _____

Hieroglyphics

Use the hieroglyphic alphabet below to decode the message.

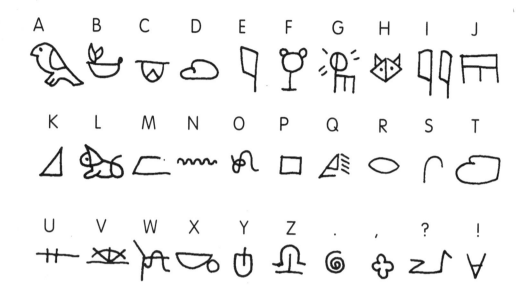

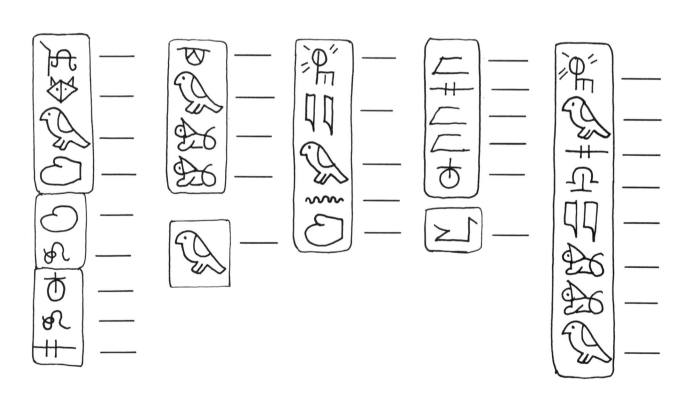

Write your own message in hieroglyphics and have a friend decode it.

Name _____

Seven Wonders of the Ancient World

Back in the days of Alexander the Great, there were seven magnificent man-made structures known as the Seven Wonders of the World. See if you can place each one in its proper location on the map according to the description by writing the number next to the correct star on the map.

1. Pyramids of Egypt at Giza were built above the desert near the banks of the Nile River as tombs for the kings.

2. Hanging Gardens of Babylon were grown on vaulted pyramid-like terraces at the palace of Babylon by the king for one of his wives, who missed the gardens of her homeland. We only know about these gardens which once existed in what we now know as Baghdad, Iraq.

3. Statue of Zeus at Olympia which stood 40 feet tall was a symbol of perfection to the Greeks, who honored Zeus as the highest god. It was neglected in Roman times and no longer stood so tall and proud.

4. The Temple of Artemis was built by King Croesus of Lydia in honor of the goddess Artemis in Ephesus on the west coast of what is Turkey today. Inside was a statue of her decorated with precious stones. It was destroyed by fire in 356 B.C. and rebuilt in 250 B.C. The second also burned.

5. The Mausoleum was built in the fourth century B.C. in the capital city of Caria, Halicarnassus, what we now know as Turkey. King Mausolus built his tomb in honor of his power. This 126' by 105', 140'-tall monument survived for centuries before it was destroyed by an earthquake.

6. The Colossus of Rhodes, built on the Island of Rhodes, was a 120-foot-tall statue of Helios, the sun god, to thank him for his protection. It also was brought down by an earthquake.

7. The Lighthouse of Alexandria, also known as the Pharos because it stood on the island of Pharos in the harbor of Alexandria, Egypt, was the first lighthouse ever built. Even though it was badly damaged by an earthquake, we have an idea of what it looked like from pictures on Roman coins.

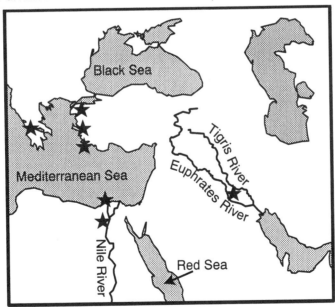

Which is the only one still standing today? _____

If you were to choose seven man-made Wonders of our World today, what would they be?_____

Name _____

How the Greeks Explain Nature

The Greeks had many myths to explain natural phenomena. See if you can find a myth to explain one of the following.

- why there are different seasons
- how we got fire
- how the world and its inhabitants were created
- why certain constellations are in the sky
- why the sun follows the same path along the sky
- why there is sickness and disease in the world
- why people fall in love

Use the space below to write one of the myths you found.

Why do you think the Greeks used myths to explain these events? _____

_____

How do we explain those same phenomena in our culture today? _____

_____

Name _____

What's in a Name?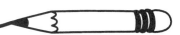

There is a Roman legend about twin boys, Romulus and Remus, grandsons of a king who was overthrown by his younger brother. Because he was afraid they might grow up and take back the kingdom, the younger brother ordered them to be drowned. They were washed up on a hill and rescued by a wolf. A shepherd found them in the wolf's den, brought them home, and raised them. When they grew up, they overthrew their wicked uncle to win back the kingdom of their grandfather. However, in a fight over which one would be king and how they would name the kingdom, Romulus killed Remus. So the city was named Rome after its first king, Romulus.

Many other cities, countries, and bodies of water were named after people, real and legendary. Can you name the person for whom each of these places was named?

_____ 1. St. Petersburg, Russia
_____ 2. Washington, D.C.
_____ 3. Alexandria
_____ 4. Ho Chi Minh City
_____ 5. Athens, Greece
_____ 6. China
_____ 7. America
_____ 8. Columbia, South America
_____ 9. Bolivia, South America
_____ 10. Houston, Texas
_____ 11. Lincoln, Nebraska
_____ 12. Hudson Bay
_____ 13. Mount St. Helens
_____ 14. Strait of Magellan
_____ 15. Lake Victoria
_____ 16. Delaware
_____ 17. Pennsylvania
_____ 18. Santa Barbara, California
_____ 19. Amazon River
_____ 20. São Paulo

A. the mother of Constantine, Emperor of Rome in the third century, Helen
B. Simón Bolívar, a Spanish conquistador
C. Abraham Lincoln, sixteenth president of the United States
D. Alexander the Great, Ancient Greek leader
E. Saint Paul, Biblical apostle
F. Lord De La Warr, governor of Virginia
G. Athena, Greek goddess
H. Saint Barbara, second century Christian martyr
I. Peter the Great, czar of Russia
J. Christopher Columbus, Spanish explorer
K. Ferdinand Magellan, Spanish explorer
L. George Washington, first president of the United States
M. William Penn, colonial leader in the United States
N. Emperor Qin or the Qin (Chin) dynasty in China.
O. Queen Victoria of Britain
P. Sam Houston, president of the republic of Texas
Q. Ho Chi Minh, Vietnamese leader
R. Henry Hudson, English explorer and sea captain
S. Amerigo Vespucci, explorer
T. legendary giant Greek women warriors

Name _____

Real Renaissance People

The era from the 1300s to the 1600s is known as the Renaissance, or the age of enlightenment, because there were so many new discoveries and inventions during this time. Today we sometimes call someone a Renaissance person if he/she has talents or abilities in many different areas, such as someone who can draw, play musical instruments, write poetry, knows a lot of information about many subjects. Listed below are some real Renaissance people who lived during the Renaissance time period. Match each name with the description telling what each was famous for accomplishing.

_____ 1. Lorenzo de Medici

_____ 2. Michelangelo

_____ 3. Leonardo Da Vinci

_____ 4. Martin Luther

_____ 5. Queen Elizabeth

_____ 6. Donatello

_____ 7. Raphael

_____ 8. Saint Thomas More

_____ 9. Machiavelli

_____10. William Shakespeare

_____11. King Charles VIII

_____12. Miguel de Cervantes

_____13. Ferdinand and Isabella

_____14. Copernicus

_____15. Galileo

a. king and queen of Spain

b. astronomer who discovered that the earth and other planets revolved around the sun

c. great sculptor, also painted the ceiling of the Sistine Chapel in Italy

d. author of "Utopia"

e. great intellect, inventor, and artist, painted **The Last Supper**

f. political and cultural leader of Florence, called "The Magnificent"

g. wrote plays, **Romeo and Juliet** and many others

h. sculptor of three statues of David

i. king of France

j. ruler of England

k. Italian astronomer who used a telescope to make discoveries about heavenly bodies

l. political leader, wrote **The Prince** about how to get power and keep it

m. wrote **Don Quixote**

n. church reformer, challenged Catholic priests

o. Italian painter of frescoes in the Vatican and also of portraits

Name _____

Can You Dig It?

Below is a sample grid of artifacts that were found at an archaeological dig. Fill in the chart with a description of each item discovered, which square(s) of the grid it was found in, and what the people who lived here probably used it for.

1 A	1 B	1 C	1 D	1 E	1 F
2 A	2 B	2 C	2 D	2 E	2 F
3 A	3 B	3 C	3 D	3 E	3 F

Grid square(s)   Item description   Use of item

_____   _____   _____
_____   _____   _____
_____   _____   _____
_____   _____   _____
_____   _____   _____
_____   _____   _____
_____   _____   _____
_____   _____   _____
_____   _____   _____

Write a paragraph describing the lifestyle of the people who lived here, based on the artifacts that were found.

Name _____

Future Finds

Suppose that 2,000 years from now someone dug up artifacts from your room. What might they find? What would they discover about you and your culture? In the boxes provided, draw five articles from your room or house and describe them and their uses as someone who is seeing them for the first time 2,000 years from now might see them.

Artifact	Description	Use
	_____	_____
	_____	_____
	_____	_____
	_____	_____
	_____	_____
	_____	_____
	_____	_____
	_____	_____
	_____	_____
	_____	_____
	_____	_____
	_____	_____
	_____	_____
	_____	_____
	_____	_____

Why might future archeologists have an easier time learning about our culture than archeologists today do learning about ancient cultures? Write your answer on the back of this page.
If this idea is interesting to you, you might want to read **Motel of Mysteries** by David Macaulay.

Name _____

Religions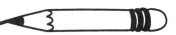

Religion has played an important role in the cultures of people since ancient times. Below are listed some of the major religions around the world. Use encyclopedias to find the information needed to fill in the chart.

Religion	symbol	holy book	leader	where it originated
Buddhism				
Hinduism				
Confucianism				
Islam (also called Muslims)				
Judaism				
Christianity				

Why do you think religion was an important part of people's cultures? _____

_____

Historical Time Line

Plot the following historical events at the proper place on the time line.

Asia:

950 B.C.	King Solomon rules Israel
400 B.C.	Confucius teaches in China
215 B.C.	Great Wall of China begins
A.D. 101	Chinese invent paper
A.D. 1271	Marco Polo explores China
A.D. 1279	Kublai Khan founds Yuan dynasty

A.D. 306	Constantine rules Roman Empire
A.D. 500	Middle Ages begin
A.D. 986	Viking explorer Eric the Red goes to Greenland
A.D. 1348	Bubonic plague hits Europe
A.D. 1448	Printing press developed

Africa:

2600 B.C.	Khufu's great pyramid begins
A.D. 970	One of the world's first universities opens in Cairo, Egypt

The Americas:

300 B.C.	City of Teotihuacán
100 B.C.	Anasazi culture in southwest United States
A.D. 250	Classic Mayan Civilization
990 B.C.	Toltec people take over Chichén Itzá, Mexico
A.D. 1200	Incas in Peru settle Cuzco
A.D. 1325	Aztecs found city of Tenochtitlan

Europe:

3000 B.C.	Huge stone structures built Stonehenge, England
900 B.C.	Etruscans settle in Italy
45 B.C.	Julius Caesar—Ruler of Rome
A.D. 100	Roman road network increases trade

3000 B.C.   2000 B.C.   1000 B.C.   B.C. 0 A.D.   A.D. 1000   A.D. 2000

1. Approximately how much time has passed from Stonehenge until now? _____
2. What was happening in Europe about the same time that King Solomon ruled Israel? _____
3. What happened in China about the same time the Romans built roads all over Europe? _____
4. Name three events that happened on three different continents in the 900s B.C. _____

156

Name _____

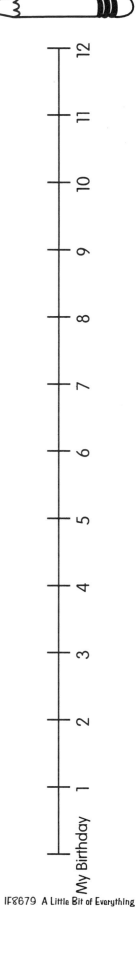

My Life Is on the Line!

Make a time line of your life by filling in the important dates and events. The numbers represent each year of your life.

1. Start with your birthday. Write the date at the beginning of the time line.

2. How old were you when you started kindergarten? If you cannot remember, you can start with this year and work backwards. If you are 11 years old and in sixth grade, you were probably ten in fifth grade and so on. Sometimes it is easier to remember important events by thinking of what happened during a particular school year.

3. Ask parents if you cannot remember how old you were for different events.

4. Some events to consider:
   when you got your first tooth
   when your siblings were born
   any contests or competitions
   special trips or vacations
   meeting a special friend
   getting a special pet or toy
   when you started walking
   when you moved
   family reunions
   awards at school or clubs
   going to a new school

5. If you don't know the exact date, use the word **circa**, a Latin word meaning "about or around."

My Birthday 1   2   3   4   5   6   7   8   9   10   11   12

IF8679 A Little Bit of Everything

Name _____

Who Said That?

Today we use expressions that refer to events or cultures of times past. After reading each description to find out the origin of each phrase, unscramble the letters to discover the phrase.

1. During the Roman empire, a vast network of roads was built which connected all of the empire to facilitate travel and trade. All the roads would get you to Rome, the center of the empire. We use an expression based on this historical fact to mean that there are many different ways to achieve the same end or get to the same place.
   lal adors dale ot moRe _____ _____ _____ _____ _____

2. The Roman Empire expanded as other nations and people were conquered by it and brought under its rule. Although many of the conquered nations were not happy about it, they soon realized that life would be much smoother if they cooperated with the Romans and did what was expected of them. We use an expression meaning when you are somewhere else, do things the way they are done in that place.
   newh ni moRe od sa het moRans od _____ ____ _____ ___ ___ ____ _____ ___.

3. The Greeks developed their own alphabet. Their language was the classic language of most of the Greek and Roman empires. If you did not know how to read or speak Greek, you wouldn't be able to understand anything. We use an expression meaning that it might as well be written in Greek because I cannot understand it at all.
   sit lal kreGe ot em _____ _____ _____ _____ _____

4. Napoleon was a powerful French revolutionary general during the late 1700s and early 1800s. Everywhere he went to battle, he won, until the Battle of Waterloo, where he was finally defeated. We use an expression based on this fact meaning that you have been defeated.
   she etm reh troWaloe ____ ____ ____ _____

5. Julius Caesar was ruler of the Roman Empire. Some of his so-called friends decided he had become too powerful and plotted to kill him. After being stabbed by several others, Julius Caesar looks up to see his most trusted friend, Brutus, ready to plunge his knife into him as well. He asks, "And you too, Brutus?" Brutus then stabs. Today we quote Julius Caesar (in Latin) when we feel we have been betrayed by someone we trusted. te ut treBu? ___ ___ _____?

6. Hernando Cortez, Spanish conquistador, attacked the mighty Aztec empire ruled by Montezuma. Although the Spanish defeated the Aztecs, many became sick with stomach ailments from drinking the water there. Some say it was Montezuma's way of getting back at the Spaniards. Today when people visit Mexico, they often have the same problem. We use this expression referring to the ancient Aztec ruler.
   zaMmotnuse veergen _____ _____

Name _____

Extra! Extra! Read All About It

Keep up to date with what is going on in the world by reading news articles. Fill in this page for each news article you read to help you sort out what is happening.

Who is involved? _____

_____

What is the major event? _____

_____

Where did it take place?_____

_____

When did it happen? _____

_____

Why? _____

_____

How did it happen? _____

_____

Any other interesting facts? _____

_____

What effects will this have on society? _____

_____

Name _____

Science Experiment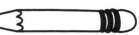

1. Question (What do I want to find out?): _____

2. Hypothesis (What do I think will happen?): _____

3. Materials needed: _____

4. Procedure (step by step):

   1. _____
   2. _____
   3. _____
   4. _____
   5. _____

Results (What did happen?) (Often a chart helps to show the results clearly):

Conclusion (What did I learn?):

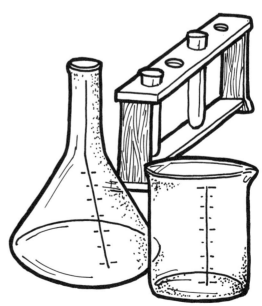

Name _____

Biome Bingo

Cut out the names of the biomes and randomly glue one in each square of the bingo grid. Cut out the plant and animal squares and place them in two separate envelopes. Use the animal cards as markers. Draw a plant card out of the envelope, for example, cactus. Find the animal that lives in the same biome, lizard, to use as a marker on the correct biome square on the grid, desert. When you have three in a row, you win. Try playing in reverse, using the plant cards as markers and the animal cards for calling.

| Biomes: | desert | rain forest | savanna | deciduous forest | |
| | marsh | ocean | tundra | coniferous forest | pond |

| Plants: | cactus | banana tree | oak tree | alpine wild flowers | |
| | pine tree | cattails | kelp | water lilies | grass |

| Animals: | lizard | mountain goat | macaw | buffalo | squirrel |
| | pinyon jay | heron | dolphin | beaver | lion |

Name _____

Building Blocks of Plants

Label the following parts of the cell.

cell wall   endoplasmic reticulum   nuclear membrane
mitochondria   nucleus   cytoplasm
chloroplast   vacuole   ribosome

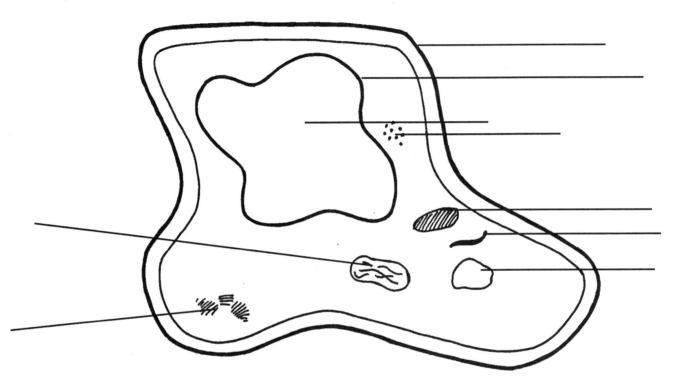

Write the name of the cell part that performs each function.

1. _____ provides shape and support
2. _____ where proteins are made
3. _____ contains chlorophyll used for photosynthesis
4. _____ moves materials within cells
5. _____ controls cell activities
6. _____ produces cell materials
7. _____ releases energy; cell powerhouse
8. _____ stores water and dissolved materials
9. _____ controls movement of materials in and out of nucleus

10. Which parts are present in plant cells that are not in animal cells? _____

Name _____

Animal Building Blocks

Label the following parts of the cell.

nucleus   cytoplasm   golgi bodies   nuclear membrane
mitochondria   endoplasmic reticulum   cell membrane   ribosome

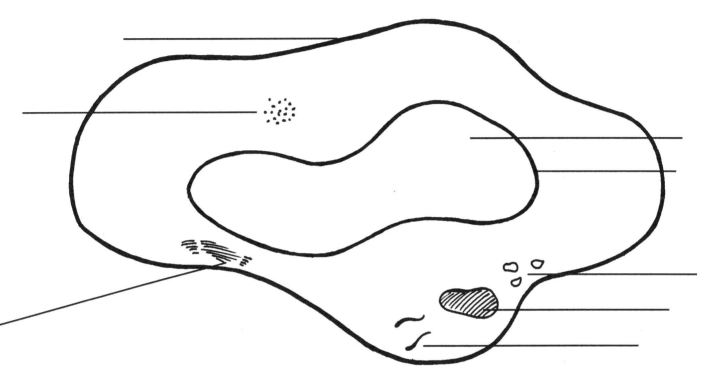

Write the name of the cell part that performs each function.

1. _____ produces cell materials
2. _____ moves materials within cells
3. _____ stores and releases chemicals
4. _____ releases energy—cell powerhouse
5. _____ where proteins are made
6. _____ controls movement of materials in and out of
                              nucleus
7. _____ controls cell activities
8. _____ controls movement of materials in and out of cell

Name _____

Now You See It, Now You Don't

1. Why do hunters wear camouflaged clothing? _____
2. Where did they learn this trick? _____

Camouflage is a defense mechanism of animals to protect them from their predators. Some animals change colors to match their surroundings. Others are spotted or striped to blend in with their environment. There are bugs that are shaped and colored like sticks or leaves so they can hide more easily.

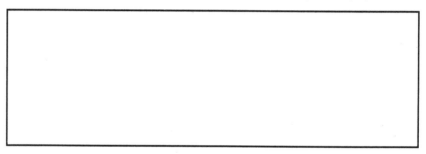

Invent a creature. It can be an insect, fish, or animal. Design a camouflage for it. In what kind of environment does it live? How will this camouflage help protect it? Draw it here:

Now draw the creature in its environment. See if a friend can find it when you are finished.

Name _____

Places, Please

Place animals from the word list into the diagrams. All reptiles will fit in the lines that form the word REPTILE, and so on. You will notice that there are more animals than places; that means some do not belong to any of the categories shown.

Word List:

abalone	anole	bowfin	cobia	conch	perch
gecko	grebe	limpet	lizard	mantid	mosquito
murre	mussel	periwinkle	scallop	skink	snail
snipe	snook	stinkpot	sulphur	tegula	terrapin
veery	whiptail				

1.   _ _ _ R _ _ _ _ _

2.   _ E _ _ _ _

3. _ _ _ _ _ _ P _ _

4.   _ _ _ _ _ T _ _ _

5.   _ _ I _ _ _

6.   L _ _ _ _ _ _

7.   _ _ _ _ E

8. _ _ _ _ F _ _

9. _ _ _ I _

10.   S _ _ _ _ _

11. _ _ _ _ _ H

12.   M _ _ _ _ _ _

13.   _ O _ _ _ _

14.   _ _ _ L _ _ _ _

15.   L _ _ _ _ _ _

16.   _ _ _ U _ _

17.   S _ _ _ _ _

18. _ _ _ _ _ _ _ _ K _ _

19.   S _ _ _ _ _ _ _

20. Into what two categories could your "leftover" animals be placed?
_____ and _____

Name _____

Label Liabilities

You probably know that in the world of chickens, a male is a rooster, a female is a hen, and a young offspring is a chick. How well do you know the labels for other animals? Below are three choices for each selected animal. Circle the letter in front of the correct answer. Labels are listed in this order: male, female, young.

1. Bear: A) bull, cow, cub   B) boar, sow, cub   C) buck, doe, cub

2. Cat: A) tom, dame, kitten   B) jack, jenny, kitten   C) tom, queen, kitten

3. Cattle: A) bull, cow, calf   B) cow, cow, calf   C) cow, sow, calf

4. Deer: A) dog, doe, fawn   B) mare, cow, fawn   C) buck, doe, fawn

5. Duck: A) cob, pen, duckling   B) drake, duck, duckling   C) cob, duck, duckling

6. Elephant: A) boar, cow, pup   B) bull, boar, cub   C) bull, cow, calf

7. Fox: A) dog, vixen, cub   B) buck, doe, pup   C) boar, sow, cub

8. Horse: A) mare, doe, pony   B) stallion, mare, foal   C) mare, stallion, foal

9. Rabbit: A) tom, queen, bunny   B) buck, doe, kit   C) jack, jenny, bunny

10. Sheep: A) ram, ewe, lamb   B) ewe, ram, lamb   C) stallion, vixen, lamb

11. Swan: A) gander, swan, duckling   B) gander, goose, gosling   C) cob, pen, cygnet

12. Swine: A) boar, pig, piglet   B) boar, sow, piglet   C) bull, sow, piglet

13. Tiger: A) tiger, tigress, cub   B) tiger, tigress, foal   C) tiger, tigret, cub

14. Whale: A) buck, doe, cub   B) boar, sow, calf   C) bull, cow, calf

Name _____

Pictures in the Sky

Name the constellations. Use the clues to help you.

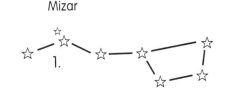

Mizar

1.

1. _____
   a. one of the brightest constellations which can be seen year-round
   b. is also known as Ursa Major, the big bear
   c. One star is really a double star, Mizar and Alcor. It was once used as an eye test.

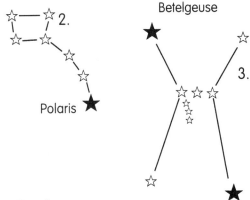

2.

Betelgeuse

3.

Polaris

2. _____
   a. contains Polaris, the North Star
   b. can be seen year-round on clear nights
   c. is also known as Ursa Minor, the Little Bear

3. _____
   a. a prominent figure in the winter sky
   b. can be seen year-round on clear nights
   c. contains a red giant star, Rigel, and a blue star, Betelgeuse.

Rigel

Deneb

4.

4. _____
   a. a summer constellation found in the Milky Way
   b. contains one of the three bright stars of the summer triangle, Deneb
   c. Although it looks like a cross, it is named for a bird.

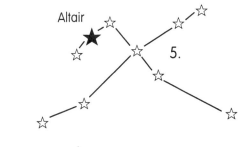

Altair

5.

5. _____
   a. contains one of the three bright stars of the summer triangle, Altair
   b. named for a bird
   c. think America

Capella

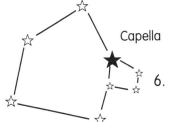

6.

6. _____
   a. Some see it as a football goal post with a football flying through, but it is actually named for a Greek charioteer.
   b. contains the second brightest star in the Northern Hemisphere, Capella
   c. It is visible in the winter sky.

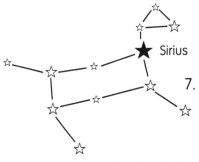

Sirius

7.

7. _____
   a. contains the brightest star in the sky
   b. There is a smaller creature of the same kind near to him in the sky.
   c. They are thought to belong to Orion, the great hunter in the sky.

167

Name _____

Royal Family in the Heavens

King Cephus and Queen Cassiopeia had a daughter, Andromeda, who was their pride and joy. She was so beautiful that they boasted she was even more beautiful than the goddesses. This made the goddesses very jealous, so they decided to destroy the whole kingdom. King Cephus pleaded with them, asking what he could do to save his kingdom. He was told there was only one way—to sacrifice his daughter. She was willing and begged him to let her go. She was tied to a rock at the edge of the sea. Just as the sea monster was coming up to get her, Prince Perseus flew by on his winged horse, Pegasus. When he saw Andromeda, he fell in love with her. He swooped down, killed the sea monster, and rescued Andromeda. They were married and the kingdom was saved from the wrath of the goddesses. To honor them for their bravery, this whole family was placed in the sky where they would live forever. You can see them in the night sky rotating around the North Star. Each of the constellations has been named for one of the characters in the story: Cephus, Cassiopeia, Andromeda, Perseus, and Pegasus. Which is which? Write the name of each constellation on the blank beside the letter.

A. _____

B. _____

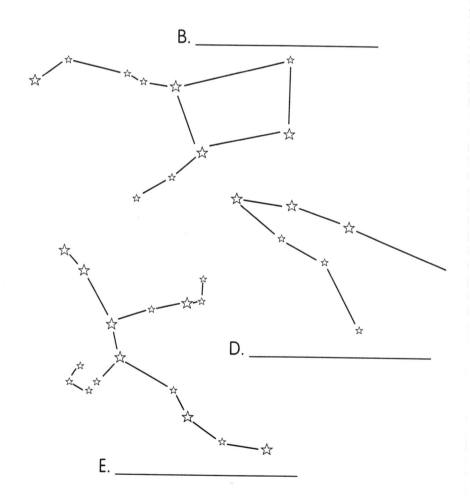

C. _____

D. _____

E. _____

The Zodiac

There are 12 constellations which follow an imaginary line around the sky called the **ecliptic**. It is the same path the sun, moon, and planets seem to follow across the sky. These constellations are called the **zodiac** from a Greek word meaning "wheel of life." Astronomers tell the location of planets by telling in which constellation each can be found. See if you can name these 12 constellations. The dates indicate the time of year when the sun rises in that constellation.

1. _____
   Dec. 15-Jan. 14
   The Archer

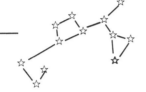

7. _____
   Jan.15-Feb. 13
   The Sea Goat

2. _____
   Feb. 14-March 14
   The Water Carrier

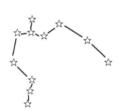

8. _____
   March 15-April 14
   The Fish

3. _____
   April 15-May 15
   The Ram

9. _____
   May 15-June 15
   The Bull

4. _____
   June 15-July 15
   The Twins

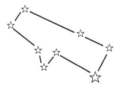

10. _____
    July 16-Aug. 15
    The Crab

5. _____
   Aug. 16-Sept. 16
   The Lion

11. _____
    Sept. 17-Oct. 16
    The Virgin

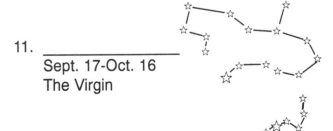

6. _____
   Oct. 17-Nov. 15
   The Scales

12. _____
    Nov. 16-Dec. 14
    The Scorpion

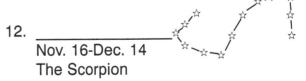

Name _____

Planetary Numbers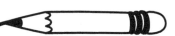

Complete the number chart by placing the digits 1 to 9 in the correct spaces in each of the first three columns. In column D, you will need other numbers. Round to the nearest day or year. You will see that in column E the numbers are filled in, but the description is missing. Can you figure out what the numbers in this column represent? Write a suitable title at the top of column E.

Planet	A. In ABC order	B. In order from the sun	C. In order from smallest to largest	D. Length of one year in earth time	E.
Mars					2
Earth					1
Pluto					1
Venus					0
Saturn					18+
Mercury					0
Uranus					15
Neptune					8
Jupiter					16

Name _____

Solar Calculations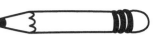

On this page you will be working with some astronomically large numbers. Round your answers to the nearest whole number or place (such as to the nearest thousand or million).

1. Write the distance from the earth to the sun in miles. _____

2. Suppose you were able to drive a car at 55 mph to the sun. How long would it take you to get to the sun:

   A. in hours? _____

   B. in days? _____

   C. in years? _____

   D. in minutes? _____

   E. in seconds? _____

3. Write your answer to 2E in word form. _____
   _____
   _____

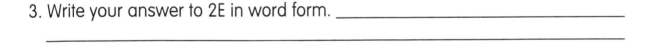

4. Now calculate the distance to the sun in:

   A. yards _____

   B. feet _____

   C. kilometers _____

   D. meters _____

5. Go back to your answer in 4C. Suppose you travelled this metric distance to the sun at a speed measured in km/h that is equal to the speed of 55 mph. Would it take more time, less time, or the same amount of time to reach the sun? _____

Name _____

Space-Age Phenomena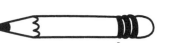

Space is full of unusual objects, weather, and phenomena. Several are hidden below as interwoven compound words or two-word phrases. Can you solve each one? Hint: The two halves of words or phrases have been placed together without changing the order of any of the letters. You may need to add an apostrophe.

Example: H A C L O L E M Y E S T   Answer: <u>HALLEY'S COMET</u>

1. B H O L A L C E K   _____

2. S N U P O E V A R   _____

3. B R A O I W N   _____

4. G R I E A N D T   _____

5. S P S U O N T S   _____

6. N E S T U T R A O R N   _____

7. S E C O L L I P A R S E   _____

8. B A S E T E R O L I T D   _____

9. N O L R I T G H E H R T N S   _____

10. D W W A H I R F T E   _____

11. S A R T U I N R G S N S   _____

12. S H O S T O T A I R N G   _____

13. T S H U T O N D R E R M   _____

14. S M E H O T E W O E R R   _____

15. F L S A R O L E A R S   _____

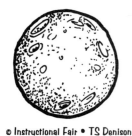

IF8679 A Little Bit of Everything

Name _____

In Your Own Words

Imagine that you are one of the very first astronauts, encountering many unusual and difficult circumstances. First, do some reading on living conditions in space, such as dealing with weightlessness, living in tight quarters, etc. Then write a first-person account of your own fictional experience on any two of the following topics. Write three or four paragraphs for each one.

1. leaving the launchpad

2. eating your first meal in outer space

3. moving about inside the space capsule

4. communicating with other crew members

5. taking a shower

6. changing your clothes

7. writing a letter

8. seeing the earth from space

9. catching your first close-up glimpse of the moon

10. walking outside the spacecraft

11. exploring the moon in a moon rover

12. docking with a foreign space vessel

13. performing scientific experiments in space

14. landing back on earth

15. deciding whether or not to make another space flight

Name _____

Ant Study

_____
Type of Ant

Choose a type of ant to study.
Draw the ant. (Label the body parts—head, thorax, and abdomen.)

Physical Characteristics: (color, size, unusual characteristics)

Habitat and food:

Life cycle/role of the queen:

Roles played by different ants in the colony:

     Guard
     Nursemaid
     Food gatherer
     Queen's attendant

Behavior: (Describe behaviors that distinguish this species from other ants.)

Name _____

Spider Web Observations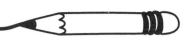

Place a web-building spider in a jar for a couple of days and observe what happens. Draw the web made by your spider.

How long did it take the spider to build the web?

_____

_____

_____

Where did the silk come from?

_____

_____

_____

Does the spider hang with its head up or down?

_____

_____

_____

Type of web _____

Explain what happens when an insect enters the web. _____

_____

_____

_____

Explain what happens when an insect enters the petri dish with a jumping (or other wandering) spider. _____

_____

_____

_____

Compare how web-building and jumping spiders attack their prey. _____

_____

_____

_____

Name _____

Symbol Sense

Forecasters use symbols to show others their weather predictions. These symbols are often used in television and newspaper forecasts. How well do you know these symbols?

The boxes below contain 12 standard weather symbols plus four "fake" symbols. At the bottom of the page are descriptions of the symbols, but there are two extra explanations. First cross out the fake symbols. Then match the real symbols with their correct labels by writing the number of each in the blank by its label. Finally, cross out the two extra explanations.

1	2	3	4
5	6	7	8
9	10	11	12
13	14	15	16

_____ A. thunderstorm

_____ B. fog

_____ C. calm

_____ D. missing data

_____ E. wind direction and speed

_____ F. drizzle

_____ G. warm front

_____ H. cold front

_____ I. ½ cloud

_____ J. snow

_____ K. no cloud

_____ L. rain shower

_____ M. mist

_____ N. high pressure system

Name _____

Keeping a Weather Chart

Using measurements that your class has gathered with its weather instruments, keep the following weather chart for several weeks, recording the information at about the same time each day. Use the notations listed below, as meteorologists do.

WEATHER CHART

Date														
Time														
Temperature														
Wind Direction														
Wind Speed														
Sky														
Barometer														
Humidity														
Precipitation														

Wind direction: N, NE, E, SE, S, SW, W, NW

Sky: O for clear, ◑ for partly cloudy, ∅ for cloudy, ⬤ for rain ◉ for snow

Barometer: ↑ for rising, ↓ for falling, —— for steady

Wind Speed: Record the number of miles per hour, as your anemometers measure the wind speed in this way.

Name _____

Search High and Low

This table shows some average high and low monthly temperatures for ten selected cities in the United States over a recent 30-year period. Search through these figures to find out the facts. The statements that are listed below the table are either true, false, or cannot be ascertained either way from the information given. If the statement is definitely true, write a T in the blank beside it. If the statement is definitely false, write an F in the blank. If the statement may or may not be true, write an M in the blank.

Average monthly temperature in degrees Fahrenheit				
City	Jan.	April	July	Oct.
Atlanta, Georgia	42	62	79	62
Austin, Texas	49	69	85	70
Chicago, Illinois	22	49	73	54
Fairbanks, Alaska	-13	30	62	25
Fargo, North Dakota	4	42	71	46
Honolulu, Hawaii	73	76	80	80
Miami, Florida	67	75	83	78
New York, New York	32	52	76	58
Portland, Maine	22	43	68	49
Richmond, Virginia	37	58	79	59

_____ 1. Of the cities shown, Fairbanks has the largest change in monthly temperature from January to July.

_____ 2. Of the cities shown, Miami has the smallest change from January to July.

_____ 3. The coldest U.S. city during the month of January is Fairbanks, Alaska.

_____ 4. The greatest variation in temperature among the cities shown between July and October occurs in Fargo.

_____ 5. During January, the temperature in New York is ten degrees warmer than in Portland.

_____ 6. Of the cities shown, Honolulu has the most constant average temperatures.

_____ 7. In Chicago, summers are 19 degrees warmer than autumns.

_____ 8. The average temperature difference in Austin from January to April is 20 degrees.

_____ 9. The average temperature in Portland during the month of July is 29 degrees warmer than the average temperature in October.

_____ 10. The range of average temperatures in April for these ten cities is 26 degrees.

_____ 11. The warmest U.S. city in July is Austin.

_____ 12. The range of average temperatures in October for these ten cities is 55 degrees.

_____ 13. The greatest range of average temperatures for these ten cities throughout the year occurs in the month of January.

_____ 14. Of these ten cities from January to October, Chicago has the biggest change in average temperature.

_____ 15. Three cities above have average temperatures in January that are 20 degrees cooler than their April average temperatures.

Name _____

Weather Trivia

Be a weather expert and find answers to all these questions. You will need reference books to help you find weather and climate facts, figures, and trivia.

1. Find the names of the four layers of the atmosphere. List them in order from closest to farthest from the surface of the earth.

   A. _____

   B. _____

   C. _____

   D. _____

2. The earth's axis is tilted at an angle of _____ degrees.

3. At the time of the spring and fall equinoxes, there are 12 hours of daylight and 12 hours of darkness all over the world. The dates of these are _____ and _____.

4. **Equinox** means _____.

5. What is an anemometer? _____

6. What does a barometer measure? _____

7. What does a hygrometer measure? _____

8. Tornadoes are most common in what country? _____ About how many are there in an average year? _____

9. Air pressure inside the funnel cloud of a tornado is extremely _____.

10. Whirlwind systems that form in the Atlantic Ocean are called _____.

11. When these form in the Far East they are called_____ or _____.

12. The three basic cloud forms are _____, _____, and _____.

13. The most common form of precipitation is _____.

14. In a high pressure weather system, the wind blows in a circle, moving in a _____ direction.

15. In which regions of the earth can thunderstorms occur nearly every day?

   _____

16. Which regions of the earth receive the heaviest snowfalls?_____

Name _____

Comparing Climates

(Each student needs two copies of this page.)

Choose two different locations in the world to compare climates.

CITY:

COUNTRY:

Latitude: Longitude:

Mark the city on the map.

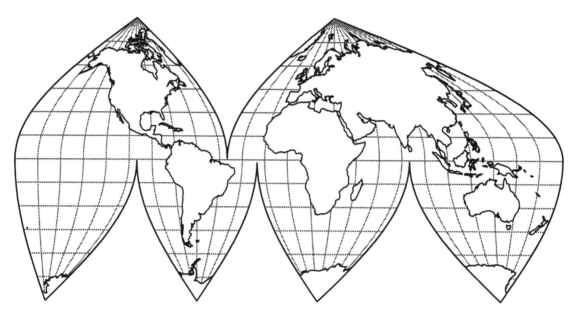

TEMPERATURE

Mark the average high and low temperatures for each month on this line graph.

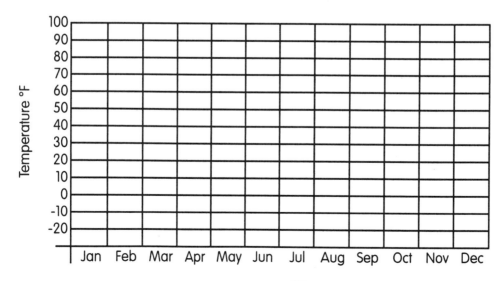

Name _____

Digging for Bones

There are 206 bones in an adult's body, but only 25 of them are hidden here. Locate the names of bones in the word search and circle them. Also, try to find four types of joints that connect bones in the human body. The words may run vertically, horizontally, or diagonally, both backwards and forwards.

```
M   A   X   I   L   L   A   R   O   P   M   E   T   C
S   U   I   D   A   R   G   H   I   N   G   E   A   A
L   A   T   N   O   R   F   Y   U   S   K   T   R   I
A   S   D   L   A   T   I   P   I   C   C   O   S   B
P   M   T   D   A   P   I   V   O   T   E   A   A   I
R   L   F   E   L   O   L   S   R   I   L   R   L   T
A   A   F   B   R   E   D   A   U   A   C   B   U   D
C   T   I   I   P   N   L   I   M   N   I   E   S   I
A   E   B   R   A   L   U   Y   E   L   V   T   A   O
T   I   U   L   E   N   O   M   F   U   A   R   C   N
E   R   L   T   M   A   N   D   I   B   L   E   R   E
M   A   A   L   U   P   A   C   S   I   C   V   U   H
B   P   S   L   A   S   R   A   T   A   T   E   M   P
C   A   R   P   A   L   S   U   R   E   M   U   H   S
```

Name _____

Bone Strength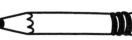

Find out whether the shape of a bone (round or flat) will affect its strength.

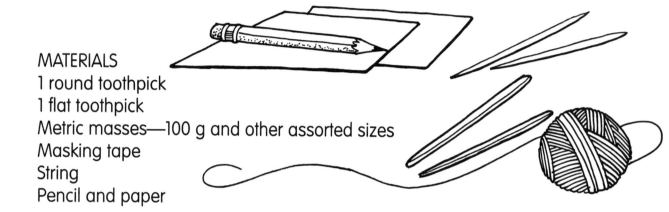

MATERIALS
1 round toothpick
1 flat toothpick
Metric masses—100 g and other assorted sizes
Masking tape
String
Pencil and paper

Flat toothpick . . . . flat bones in your body like ribs

Round toothpick . . . . . round bones in the body like arm and leg bones

PROCEDURE

1. Tape one round toothpick and one flat toothpick to the edge of a table so half of each toothpick extends over the edge of the table. Press down on the tape to be certain they stay in place.

2. Using string, hang masses of the same size on the end of each toothpick. Start with 100 g and keep adding masses until the toothpick breaks.

3. Observe which toothpick bends the most as you add weight. Write down the mass at which each toothpick breaks.

4. Conclusions:
   Which shape bones provide better support? _____
   Which bones provide better protection? _____
   Which bones best resist injury? _____

human body

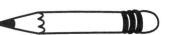

The Shrink Test

Name _____

AM   PM

Measure your height each day when you first get up in the morning and when you go to bed at night. Record the measurements on the chart.

Date	Morning	Evening	Difference

What was the greatest difference in height in a single day? _____

What was the smallest difference in a single day?_____

What was the average difference in height over seven days? _____

Make a bar graph to show the differences in height each day.

Name _____

Making a Model Lung

This model lung will show you
what happens when you breathe.

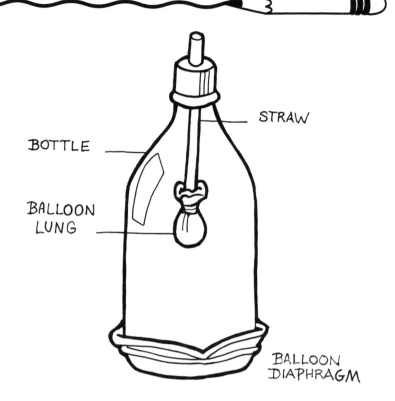

BOTTLE

STRAW

BALLOON
LUNG

BALLOON
DIAPHRAGM

MATERIALS
Plastic liter soda bottle
Balloons
Clay
Large, sturdy straw
Scissors
Thick rubber bands

PROCEDURE

1. Punch a hole in the lid of your bottle and
   insert a straw.

2. Make the straw airtight in your bottle by
   placing clay around the edges of the straw
   and bottle top.

3. Remove the bottom of the bottle by cutting it away with scissors.

4. Cut open a balloon so you have a rectangular piece of rubber. Fasten this piece of
   rubber to the bottom of the bottle with a rubber band. The rubber should be stretched
   tight.

5. Attach another small, thin balloon to the end of the straw that will be inside your bottle.

6. Put the bottle top with the straw inserted into your bottle. Be certain it is on tight.

7. Press in on the balloon (the diaphragm) at the bottom of your bottle. Watch as the lung
   (balloon inside) contracts. With your other hand, feel the air that comes out of the straw
   at the top. Repeat this action so you can see the lung contract and then relax. . .
   contract and relax.

Name _____

Skin Appearance & Evaporation

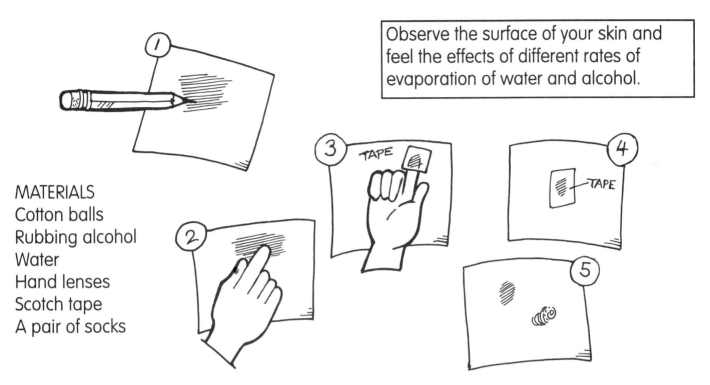

> Observe the surface of your skin and feel the effects of different rates of evaporation of water and alcohol.

MATERIALS
Cotton balls
Rubbing alcohol
Water
Hand lenses
Scotch tape
A pair of socks

PROCEDURE

1. Using a hand lens, examine the skin on the back of your hand, noticing the pores and creases. Then, look at the skin on the palm of your hand. Are there any differences? On the back of this page, draw a picture showing how the skin looks.

2. Make some skin prints by rubbing some soft pencil lead onto a paper. Place your finger into the lead. Place a piece of Scotch tape over your finger and pull it away. Then press the Scotch tape onto a clean sheet of paper. See how many skin prints you can find. Place some of them on the back of this page.

3. Dip one cotton ball into water and another into rubbing alcohol. Blindfold your partner and put alcohol on one wrist and water on the other. Which one feels cooler? (Alcohol evaporates more quickly than water.)

4. On a very hot day, take one sock of a pair and soak it in water. Squeeze the sock out and put the damp sock on one foot and the dry sock on the other foot. Do you feel any difference?

> FIND OUT more about fingerprints and how they are used to solve crimes!

Name _____

Mapping Your Hand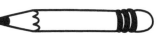

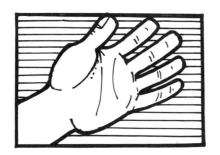

Some spots on your skin are more sensitive than others because they contain more nerve endings. Find out which places on your hand are the most sensitive.

MATERIALS
Fine-tip black marking pen
Dull pencil
Straight pin
Wet frozen string
Paper clip immersed in boiling water
Sheet of chart paper

			X
	√		
O			
		•	√

√	hot	•	pressure
X	cold	O	pain

PROCEDURE

1. Draw a two-inch square on the back of your hand with a fine-tip marker. Divide it into 16 equal squares.

2. On chart paper, make a square divided into 16 equal parts like the one on your hand. This one can be much larger.

3. First, touch each square on your hand with the tip of a pin. Mark an x in each square on the chart that corresponds to the square where you felt the pin. The pin is a pain sensor.

4. Next, touch each square on your hand with the dull pencil. This is the pressure sensor. Mark the corresponding squares on the chart, wherever you felt the pencil.

5. Repeat this process with the frozen string (cold sensor) and the hot paper clip (heat sensor). Mark the squares on the chart appropriately.

6. Observe from your chart which areas were most sensitive to each of the sensors.

Try this test on the palm of your hand. Instead of drawing a square, just test the palm of your hand in different areas with each sensor. Is the palm more sensitive than the back of your hand? Why?

Name _____

Sickly Sleuthwork

You have probably heard of most of the diseases listed below, but how much do you know about them? In the blank next to each disease, write the letter that tells what part(s) of the body this disease primarily affects. Some letters will be used more than once. Two letters will not be used at all.

____ 1. multiple sclerosis

____ 2. tuberculosis

____ 3. influenza

____ 4. AIDS

____ 5. cholera

____ 6. impetigo

____ 7. arthritis

____ 8. leukemia

____ 9. colitis

____ 10. glaucoma

____ 11. rheumatic fever

____ 12. hepatitis

____ 13. osteoporosis

____ 14. shingles

____ 15. diabetes

____ 16. dysentery

____ 17. goiter

A. kidney

C. eye

D. white blood cells

E. respiratory system (throat, lungs, etc.)

L. ear

N. thyroid gland

O. digestive system (stomach, intestines, pancreas, liver, etc.)

R. skeletal system (bones, joints, etc.)

S. central nervous system (brain, nerves, spinal cord)

T. heart

U. skin

Y. immune system

If you have solved this puzzle correctly, you will be able to read a piece of medical advice should you contract any alarming symptoms!

Name _____

Circuit Cards

Use these circuit cards to complete a circuit and light the bulb. This will help you figure out how the wires are connected inside the card.

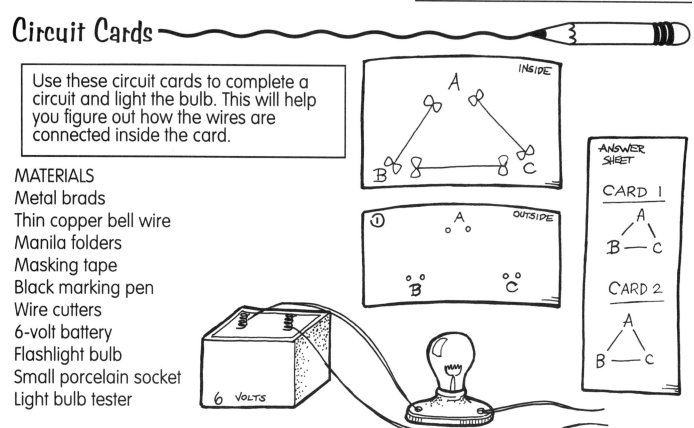

MATERIALS
Metal brads
Thin copper bell wire
Manila folders
Masking tape
Black marking pen
Wire cutters
6-volt battery
Flashlight bulb
Small porcelain socket
Light bulb tester

PROCEDURE

1. Cut each folder into a rectangular shape, cutting off the uneven edges.

2. Push two brads through the folder at each end of a triangle as shown above.

3. On the outside of the card, mark one point of the triangle with A, one with B, and one with C.

4. On the inside of the card, attach a piece of wire from A to B, B to C, or C to A. The wire may be attached along one of these paths, two of these paths, or all three. Make each card different.

5. Number each card and write down how the wires are attached on the inside on a separate sheet of paper.

6. Close the card with the wires on the inside and tape the edges shut with masking tape.

7. Using a battery and light bulb tester as shown above, test each circuit card to see where the wires are attached inside the card. Touch a wire to A and a wire to B. If the bulb lights, there is a wire on the inside of the card from A to B. The bulb lights because you are completing the circuit.

Name _____

Before

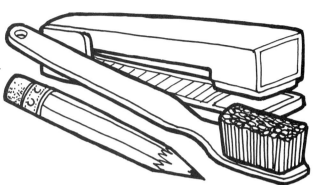

Do you ever wonder how people lived before today's modern conveniences—both major and minor? Here is a chance to think and write about a few specific circumstances. Be as practical or as creative as you like as you answer the following questions. Write a paragraph for each question on another sheet of paper.

1. The toothbrush was invented in 1498, and the toothpaste tube in 1892. Do you think toothpaste was used before 1892? If so, how was it sold, handled, and used? What was toothpaste like back then?

2. On another dental topic, forceps used for extracting teeth were invented in 1525. What do you think happened before that? Were teeth not pulled? Or were they pulled with something else? What?

3. Printed books were used as early as A.D. 868 in China. But page numbers in printed books were not used until 1470. What problems would that present? How did people refer to specific book excerpts without page numbers?

4. Numbers were used thousands of years ago—long before the time of Christ. But mathematical signs came much later: + and - in 1489; = in 1557; x in 1631, and so on. How did people write math sentences before then? What difficulties might they have had?

5. Graphite pencils were introduced in 1565. Erasers made of India rubber were invented in 1770. In between those years, how were mistakes corrected? What materials might have been used?

6. The stapler was invented in 1868 and the paper clip in 1900. Before then, how did people keep their papers organized? How might they have attached several pages together?

7. Theater curtains were first used in 1664 in Japan. How would theatrical performances have been different before then, without the curtains?

Name _____

It's Your Turn

The world is just waiting for a brilliant new invention—from you! Here are some bizarre ideas to help you get started. Work on a few that interest you and then focus on your best idea. Write a one-page description of your new invention. Include information on your item's purpose, construction, marketability, and cost. Also include a drawing and a sample magazine advertisement for your new invention.

Sample Ideas for New Inventions:

1. a futuristic, energy-efficient building for work, recreation, or living

2. a safe and fascinating new toy for babies

3. a hat for people with unruly hair

4. another way to construct books

5. the latest comfort inside a car

6. a re-invented wheel

7. a unique transportation device

8. the all-improved hamster cage

9. a new form of communication

10. a gadget to assist your teacher in all the daily work

11. a musical instrument

12. a new kitchen tool for chopping, slicing, or dicing

13. a new method for building roads

14. all-purpose shoes

15. a new piece of exercise equipment

16. a new idea in home decorating

17. luggage everyone will want to take on their next vacation

18. the necktie that does more

Name _____

Preposterous Publicity

These news stories could not possibly be accurate, because, on the date given, one of the items mentioned was not yet invented. In the blank below each story, write the item that is out of place, along with its date of origin, if possible.

A. Tuner Trips: June 13, 1765

Last Thursday, Mr. Keith Fisher, local piano tuner, was injured at the home of a client, Mrs. Diana Nixon. Mr. Fisher completed the tuning and put his tuning fork away. Since it was a sweltering 88° F, Mrs. Nixon then offered the tuner a cold glass of fizzy mineral water. As Mr. Fisher reached for the glass, he slipped on little Timmy's roller skates, sending the water across the jigsaw puzzle on the table and sending Mr. Fisher's forehead into Mrs. Nixon's metal sewing scissors. After Dr. Blechl arrived and treated Mr. Fisher's wound, Mrs. Nixon fed both the tuner and Timmy a sandwich and sent the boy to kindergarten.

Answer: _____ Correct year_____

B. Bank Break-In: April 25, 1950

A burglary was reported at the city's All-Saver's Drive-In Bank last night. Billy Jones, who was riding down Hill Street on his skateboard, reported seeing a man in a dark-hooded coat running from the building about 6 p.m. Police officers said the burglar gained entrance to the bank when he threw a can of window polish through the glass pane on the front door and reached through the frame and unlocked the handle. Bank officials stated that all money was secured in the vault. The only items reported missing were these from the bank president's office: an electric guitar left by his teenage daughter and an espresso coffee machine, which had been a Christmas present from his wife. Police continue to look for suspects who may have known the family and were aware that these items were being kept in the bank office.

Answer: _____ Correct year_____

Name _____

Keyboard Quest

Knowing the computer keyboard is essential to quickly and accurately entering data. Here are some activities to help you learn the location of letters.

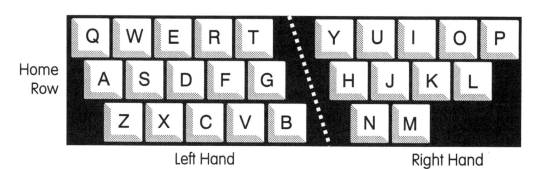

Home Row

Left Hand   Right Hand

Find words to complete this chart. Spell words using letters typed with just the right hand, the left hand, the home-row keys, or those that alternate left and right (or right- and left-hand) keys. WARNING: It may not be possible to complete all the boxes. You are allowed to repeat letters within words. One word in each row has been filled in as an example.

	5 words of 4 letters	3 words of 5 letters	2 words of 6 or more letters	longest word possible
A. Left-hand keys	beat			
B. Right-hand keys	hill			
C. Home-row keys	hall			
D. Alternating keys	with			

Name _____

Chip, Chip Hooray!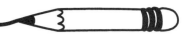

Electrical pulses do all the work inside a computer. The pulses are controlled by electronic components. In the first computers, these components were glass valves, which used a lot of power, grew very hot, and were unreliable. Next came the smaller and cheaper transistors. They used much less power and stayed cooler.

But, in the 1960s, the development of the silicon chip revolutionized the construction of computers. The integrated circuit, or "chip," is a tiny slice of silicon on which millions of components are packed closely together. With the chip, it is now possible to build smaller, faster computers than ever before.

To find out how these amazing chips are made, place the steps below in chronological order. If you read the steps carefully and use some logic, you should be able to sequence them correctly. Number the steps from 1 to 10 in the order in which they must be performed.

_____ 1. The chips are then tested to see if an electric current can pass through each circuit.

_____ 2. The silicon is sliced into thin wafers. Later, up to 500 chips will be made from each wafer.

_____ 3. The silicon wafers are placed in a furnace at a temperature of over 1800°F.

_____ 4. The different circuits are built up, one on top of the other, in the silicon wafer. The circuits are designed using a computer and drawn up to 250 times larger than they will be on the finished chip.

_____ 5. After being cut, the chips are again inspected. Faulty ones are thrown away.

_____ 6. Crystals of pure silicon are grown in a vacuum oven. The silicon is so pure that it will not conduct electricity until treated with certain chemicals.

_____ 7. The wafer is cut into individual chips by a diamond or a laser saw.

_____ 8. Each tiny chip is placed inside a plastic case with gold wires connecting the circuits to the pins in the case.

_____ 9. In the intense heat of the furnace, atoms of certain chemicals enter the surface of the silicon, along the printed lines of the circuit.

_____ 10. The circuit designs are then reduced to the size of the chip and printed one at a time onto the silicon wafer.

Name _____

Newton's Laws

A scientist named Isaac Newton experimented and developed three laws of motion that hold true for matter on earth.

Law 1: An object in motion will remain in motion, and an object at rest will remain at rest, unless a net force acts on it.

Law 2: Acceleration of an object increases as the amount of force causing acceleration increases. The bigger the mass of the object, the larger the force needed to produce acceleration.

Law 3: For every action there is an equal and opposite reaction.

Below are examples of motion. On the line next to the number, write the number of the law that is being demonstrated.

_____ 1. You blow up a balloon and then let it go. The balloon flies forward as the air rushes out the back.

_____ 2. You are in a car moving at a steady pace down the road. The driver slams on the breaks and stops the car suddenly. Unless you have your seat belt on, you fly forward.

_____ 3. You swing the baseball bat and hit the ball, but it doesn't go as far as when your dad swung the bat faster.

_____ 4. You push a wheelbarrow full of rocks to the spot where your mom wants to build a rock garden and dump them out. Pushing the empty wheelbarrow back to the garage is much easier.

_____ 5. You are standing on a bus waiting for it to start. When it starts, you fall backward.

_____ 6. You are in a swimming pool gripping on to the edge. You push off the wall with your feet and shoot forward in the water.

_____ 7. You are on a sailboat in the water. It is not moving because there is no wind. Suddenly the wind begins to blow and the boat moves forward.

_____ 8. You are playing football and easily push your skinny opponent out of the way. But for the next play, they substitute a larger player. You push harder and harder and can barely get him to budge.

_____ 9. You are shooting a 22 rifle at a target. You release the trigger and the gun kicks back into your shoulder as the bullet goes forward.

_____ 10. You are playing marbles. You shoot one marble into another. The one you shot stops, but the one it hit moves out of the circle.

Name _____

Drawing Atoms

Atoms are composed of a positively charged nucleus surrounded by negatively charged shells of electrons. Within the nucleus are protons (positive charge +) and neutrons (no charge). The number of electrons (-) always equals the number of protons. Then the atom is balanced. There is no electrical charge. The first electron shell can hold two electrons. If it is full and there are remaining electrons, they move to the second shell. The second electron shell can hold eight electrons. The third shell also holds eight electrons.

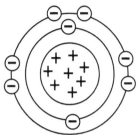

Here is a drawing of an oxygen atom. It has eight protons (+) in the nucleus. It has eight electrons (-) in the shells. First the inside shell is filled with two electrons. The other six are in the outer shell.

Draw atoms of each of the following elements with the correct number of protons in the nucleus and the correct number of electrons in each surrounding shell. The number in parentheses tells you how many protons and electrons each element contains.

hydrogen (1)　　　　　carbon (6)　　　　　calcium (20)

nitrogen (7)　　　　　chlorine (17)　　　　　sodium (11)

Name _____

How Fit Are You?

There are four different kinds of exercise:
1. flexibility: the range of movement of joints
2. muscle strength: the ability to exert force against resistance
3. muscle endurance: the ability of muscles to keep working over a period of time without causing fatigue
4. heart and lung endurance: the ability of lungs and heart to keep working efficiently during long periods of vigorous activity.

Test your ability in each of these areas:
1. Flexibility: Sit on the floor with legs straight in front. Heels should touch a line on the floor about 5" apart. Place a yard stick on the floor between legs with the 15" mark even with your heels. Slowly reach as far forward as possible and hold. Record the most distant reach on the stick.

Male	Female	Rating
22+	23+	excellent
17-21	20-22	good
13-16	17-19	average
9-12	14-16	fair
8 or less	13 or less	poor

your score: _____

your rating: _____

2. Muscle Strength: Do a standing long jump. Land on both feet. Compare the distance with your height.

Less than your height: poor
Equal to your height: Fair
2"-4" more than your height: good
5"-9" more than your height: excellent

distance: _____

rating: _____

3. Muscle Endurance: Do as many sit-ups as you can in one minute.

Male	Female	Rating
40	30	excellent
33-39	24-29	good
29-32	18-24	average
21 -28	11 -17	fair
less than 21	less than 11	poor

number of sit-ups _____

rating _____

4. Heart and Lung Endurance: Step up and down a stair step at the rate of 24 per minute. Check your pulse when you are finished.

70-80	excellent
81-105	good
106-111	average
120-130	fair
131+	poor

your pulse: _____

rating: _____

Set an exercise program for yourself to improve in the areas where your rating was not as good as you would like it to be.

Name _____

What's for Dinner?

Cut out the cards below and glue each one onto a 3" by 5" index card. You may illustrate the cards. You will use these cards to play a game for two to four players. Object of the game: To collect the correct cards in each category to make a balanced diet. How to play: Shuffle the cards and deal out all the cards. If only two are playing, use only half the deck. Be certain to use half the cards from each category. Players may trade cards in groups of one, two, three, or four cards in the same category by holding out the cards they want to trade and calling out the number of cards in the group. A player may trade with anyone else who is trying to trade the same number of cards. Cards in the sweets category or the wild cards may be used with any group. The wild cards can take the place of any other card. To win: A player must collect the following cards: Breads: between 6 and 11; Vegetables: between 3 and 5, Fruit: between 2 and 4; Proteins: between 2 and 3, Dairy: between 2 and 3, and 1 or less Sweets. When a player collects the correct cards, he/she calls out "dinner time!" and the play ends.

fruit apple	fruit orange	fruit banana	fruit pear	fruit peach	fruit plum
fruit kiwi	fruit mango	veggie peas	veggie corn	veggie lettuce	veggie green beans
veggie cabbage	veggie spinach	veggie carrots	veggie celery	veggie broccoli	veggie cucumbers
veggie cauliflower	veggie zucchini	proteins chicken	proteins hamburger	proteins steak	proteins refried beans
proteins pork chops	proteins peanut butter	proteins eggs	proteins ham	dairy milk	dairy yogurt
dairy cheese	dairy ice cream	dairy cream cheese	dairy cottage cheese	dairy sour cream	dairy chocolate milk
breads toast	breads cereal	breads rice	breads pasta	breads potatoes	breads pancakes
breads waffles	breads dinner rolls	breads corn bread	breads bagel	breads crackers	breads granola bar
breads pretzels	breads rice cakes	breads popcorn	breads oatmeal	breads macaroni	breads tortillas
breads corn chips	breads blueberry muffins	breads sourdough bread	breads banana bread	breads whole wheat bread	breads hamburger buns
sweets candy bar	sweets cookies	sweets jawbreaker	sweets bubble gum	WILD	WILD

Name _____

It's Hot to Not

Design a bumper sticker, button, and radio advertisement to persuade people not to smoke.

Radio Add:

_____

_____

_____

_____

_____

Name _____

Dear Aunt Sally—Help!

Pretend that you are Aunt Sally, the editor of a help column in a newspaper for teens. How would you answer each of these letters?

Dear Aunt Sally,
My friend invited me to a party at his house next weekend while his parents are out of town. I know there will be drinking. What should I do? I don't want to look like a nerd because I'm scared to go.

From, Wanna-be-Cool

Dear Aunt Sally,
My friend got some marijuana from her older sister. She says we ought to try it, that just doing it once won't hurt. Is she right?

From, Curious

Dear Aunt Sally,
I know there are kids in my school who do drugs and I know where they get them from. Should I tell someone? I'm afraid no one will like me if I tell.

From, ?

Dear Aunt Sally,
I started smoking last year because my friends were all doing it. I used to be a good soccer player, but now I have a hard time running. I thought it might be from the smoking, so I tried to quit, but I get shaky and something tells me I need to have a cigarette. What should I do?

From, Scared

Name _____

Blown Away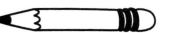

Fill in the chart below by describing each natural disaster and the steps you should take to be safe.

	What is it?	What should you do?
Hurricane		
Tornado		
Blizzard		
Earthquake		
Electrical Storm		

Choose one of the disasters and prepare a skit to show your class what to do in that situation.

What Would You Do?

Consult a first-aid book to describe what you would do in each of the following first-aid situations.

1. You are sitting at the dinner table and your little brother starts choking on his food. He is still able to breathe. What will you do?

2. You are playing basketball on a hot summer day. One of your friends sits down and says he doesn't feel well. You notice that he is not sweating. What do you do?

3. You and your friend are roller blading. She falls and cuts her hand badly on a piece of broken glass. What do you do?

4. You and your two best friends are on a mountain bike ride a mile away from any houses. Your friend falls and lands on her arm. When she leans on it to get up she screams in pain as it collapses under her. The skin is not broken, but the arm looks misshapen. What will you do?

5. You are cooking macaroni and cheese for you and your sister. She wants to help and pulls the pan of boiling water down. It spills all over her arm and burns it. What will you do?

6. You and your friend are skiing on a very cold day. She drops a mitten from the chair lift into the trees below. As you are skiing down, she tells you she doesn't have any feeling in her fingers. The fingertips are white. What will you do?

7. You and your friends are building a tree fort in your yard after school. Your friend slips and falls to the ground. You call and he does not answer. When you climb down, you find he is unconscious. What will you do?

8. You are playing soccer and one of the players has a seizure. You have heard he has epilepsy. What will you do?

9. Your scouting troop has been hiking for a couple of hours. The boy walking in front of you stops and seems disoriented. You notice a bracelet on his wrist saying he is diabetic. What should you do?

10. You and your dad are playing catch. You notice he is short of breath and you tease him about being out of shape. He is rubbing his right arm and says he needs to sit down a minute. He has pains in his chest. What should you do?

Name _____

Music and Math Connections

Did you know that there are many similarities between music and math? One similarity is that they both use symbols, many of which you see below. Use the Venn diagram to separate them into categories, the music symbols on the left, the math symbols on the right and any symbols that are used for both in the middle section. For an extra challenge, research what each symbol represents.

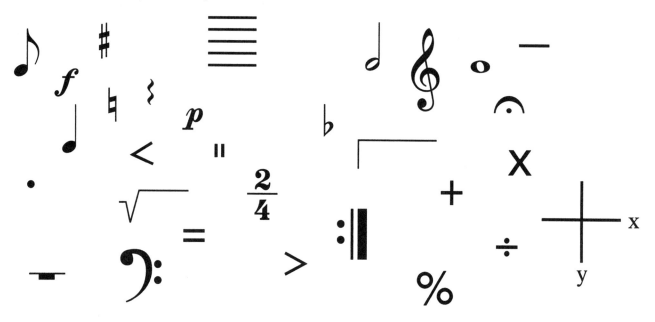

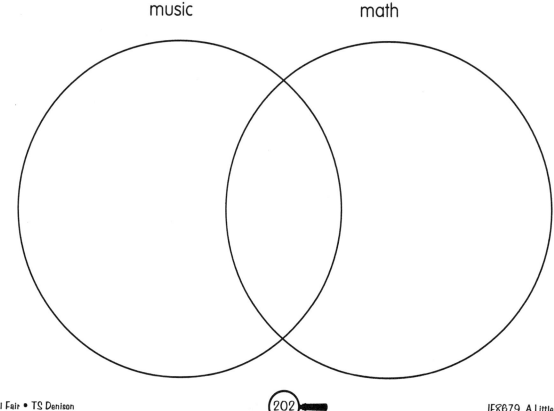

music   math

202

Name _____

Musical Words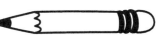

Did you know that you can spell words with musical notes? Use the staff below to help find the correct letter for each note.

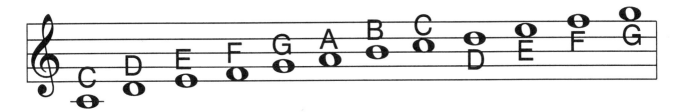

Write the correct letter on the space below each note to find the words that are spelled by the notes.

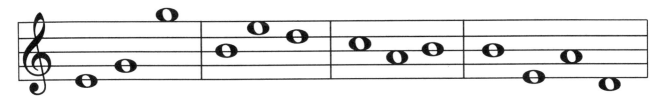

— — — —   — — — —   — — — —   — — — —

Draw notes on the correct lines and spaces to spell the following words.

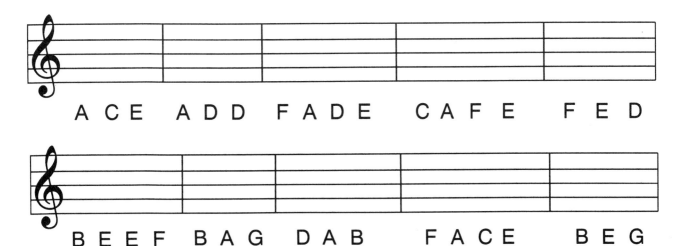

A C E   A D D   F A D E   C A F E   F E D

B E E F   B A G   D A B   F A C E   B E G

Name _____

I Believe in Music

Cut the list of words into cards. Divide the class into two or three teams. Draw the first card and read the word or phrase out loud. The first team must think of a song that contains that word and sing at least seven words of the song. Then team two must think of a song using the same word. Continue through all the teams and then go back to team one again. If a team cannot think of a song, it is out for that round. Continue with the same word until there is only one team left. That team wins that round. Start the next word with team two and continue in the same way until you run out of time. Each song may be used only once in each round, but may be used again for a different round. Example: "Row, Row, Row your boat gently down the stream" may be used for a vehicle (boat), a body of water (stream), and dream ("life is but a dream"). The blank cards are for you to add your own words to the game.

heart	any color	a celestial object
dream	any animal	name of city, state, country
day	any number	name of a historical figure
flag	any vehicle	a family member (mom, dad)
bell(s)	any fruit	any form of the word **go**
smile	any flower	a body of water
walk	a body part	name of clothing
friend	any building	name of a holiday

Name _____

Great Composers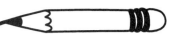

Fill in the blanks below by selecting the composer and a song he has written to match the fun facts about the musicians' lives.

Songs:
"Brandenburg Concertos"   "Farewell Symphony"   "Lullaby"
"Eine klein Nachtmusick"   "Nutcracker Suite"   "Ode to Joy"

Musicians:
Ludwig van Beethoven   Wolfgang Amadeus Mozart   Johann S. Bach
Peter I. Tchaikovsky   Joseph Haydn   Johannes Brahms

Fun Facts:

1. This composer learned to play the violin at age three and was composing music at age five. By age six he was touring Europe playing music for royalty. He never attended school, but learned to speak 15 languages.

   Name: _____ song _____

2. Came from a family of musicians. In fact there were 53 of them with the same name. Both his parents died by the time he was ten. He was once thrown in jail by his employer and wrote 46 music pieces while there. One of his most loved music pieces today was written as a job application, but he didn't get the job. He was blind in his last years.

   Name: _____ song _____

3. His father was a singer and taught him to play the violin and piano. By age twelve he supported his family by publishing music and playing the organ. He became deaf in his twenties, but still continued to compose music.

   Name: _____ song _____

4. The last of the three Ebbs. He grew up in the slums of Hamburg, Germany. At his first performance of one of his concertos, everyone hissed. He is most well known for a song you probably heard as a young child.

   Name: _____ song _____

5. This musician loved to play practical jokes. He conducted an orchestra for a prince in Austria. The musicians were overdue for a vacation, so to remind the prince, the conductor wrote a symphony where each musician left one by one until there was only one left playing. He too turned off his light and walked away. It worked. They got their vacation.

   Name: _____ song _____

6. He was the first Russian composer to receive systematic training in music. He wrote his most cheerful music when he was depressed. A woman he never met paid him so he could compose music. He is most well known for his ballet music.

   Name: _____ song _____

Name _____

Creativity

Exercise your brain and see how creative you can be. Turn the shape below into a picture. Before you start drawing, take time to think of all the possibilities. Turn your paper and look at it from all directions. Rather than using your first idea, see if you can think of something unusual that no one else would draw. Now draw your picture. Compare it with your classmates' pictures to see how many different ideas were used.

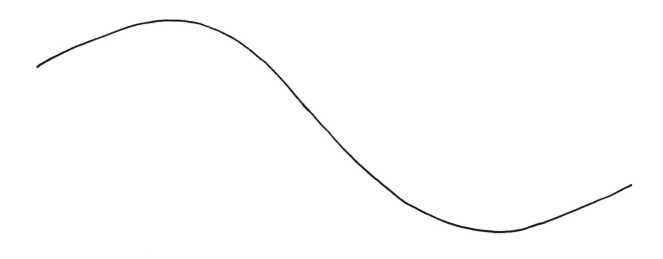

Try again with one of these shapes:

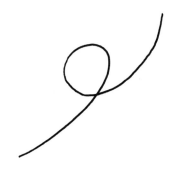

Name _____

Color Wheel

Artists use color wheels to help them understand how colors work together. The circles labeled with P represent the three primary colors. Color them red, blue, and yellow. The circles in between represent secondary colors, which are made by mixing the two primary colors on either side. Mix the two primary colors on both sides of each "s" circle to find three secondary colors.

To personalize your color wheel, cut the color circles into shapes and glue them onto a separate paper. Be certain to keep them in the same order. (Examples: blobs of paint on an artist's palette, fish in an aquarium).

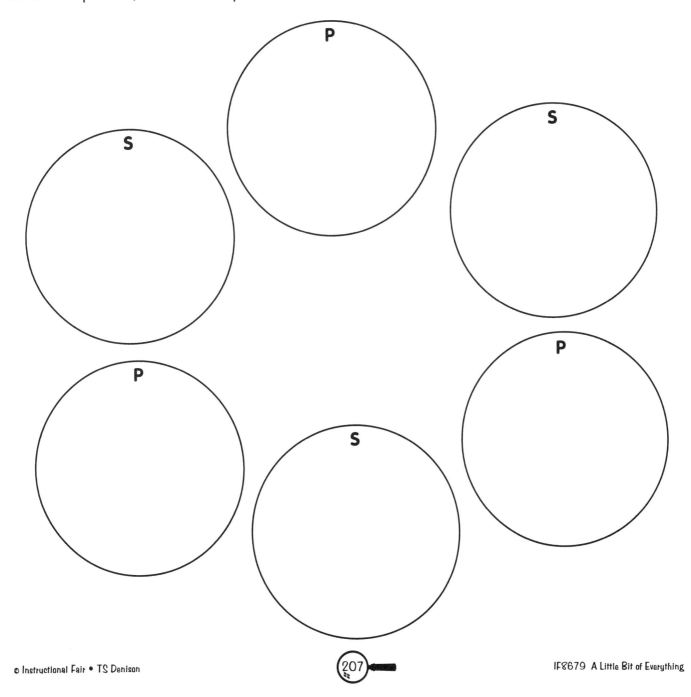

Name _____

Complementary Colors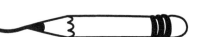

Two colors directly opposite each other on the color wheel are complementary. They include one primary and one secondary color. What are the three sets of complementary colors?

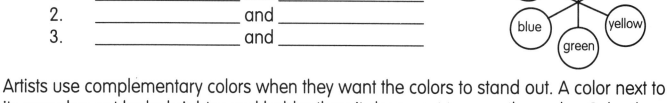

1. _____ and _____
2. _____ and _____
3. _____ and _____

Artists use complementary colors when they want the colors to stand out. A color next to its complement looks brighter and bolder than it does next to any other color. Color the boxes below according to the directions.

Color dot red, background green

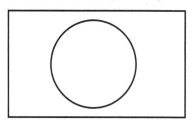

Color dot orange, background blue

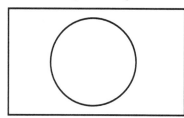

Color dot yellow, background purple

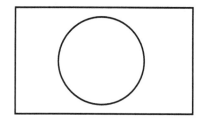

Color dot red, background orange

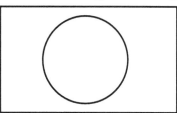

Color dot orange, background yellow

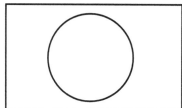

Color dot yellow, background green

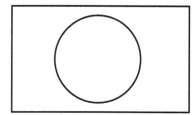

In which does the red dot appear brighter? _____ The orange dot? _____
The yellow dot?_____

In the space below, draw a design and color it using two complementary colors.

Mystery Picture

The boxes in the grids are numbered, but the grid on the left is all mixed up! To discover the mystery picture, color each box in the empty grid exactly like the box in the left grid with the corresponding number.

Name _____

1	2	3	4
5	6	7	8
9	10	11	12
13	14	15	16

Name _____

Positive and Negative Are More Than Math Symbols

When we hear the words **positive** and **negative**, we usually think of math. But artists also use those words. Positive space refers to the objects in a picture and negative space is the background shape. Both are equally important. Choose two contrasting colors. Color the 1s with the first color and the 2s with the second color. In half of the picture squares, the 1s are the positive space, and the 2s are the negative space. In the other half of the pictures, it is the opposite.

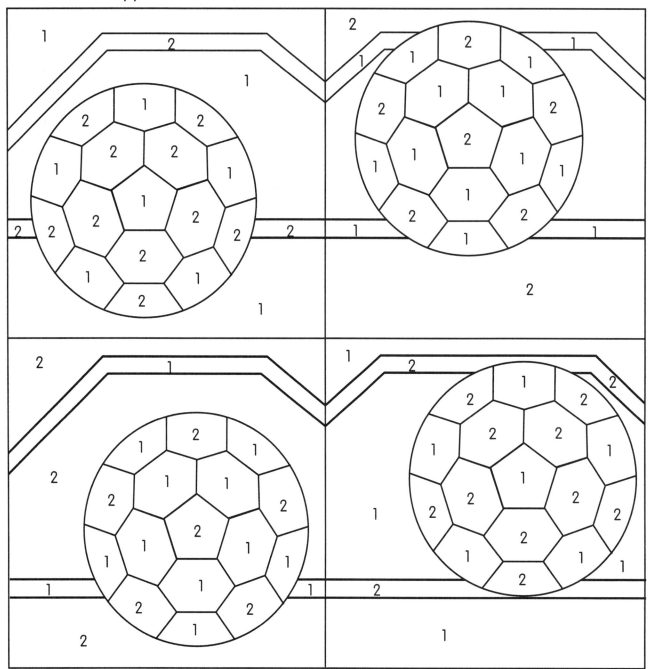

Try a design of your own!

art

Shading Shapes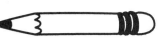

Use a pencil to shade each of the geometric shapes. The arrow shows the light source. Use the small pictures as examples. Each of the shapes can be found in objects in the world around us. Some of these are listed. Can you think of others?

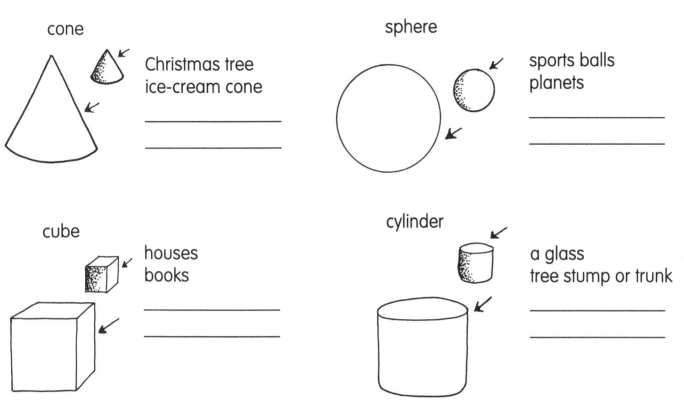

cone

Christmas tree
ice-cream cone

_____
_____

sphere

sports balls
planets

_____
_____

cube

houses
books

_____
_____

cylinder

a glass
tree stump or trunk

_____
_____

Choose an object that has one of these shapes to draw below. Shade it the same way you did above to give your object the appearance of having depth.

Name _____

Portrait Drawing

Place a sheet of paper over this page and lightly trace over the guidelines to draw a portrait. The lines will help you to draw the facial features in the proper place and proportion. Add facial features and hair of your choice. When you are finished, erase the guidelines.

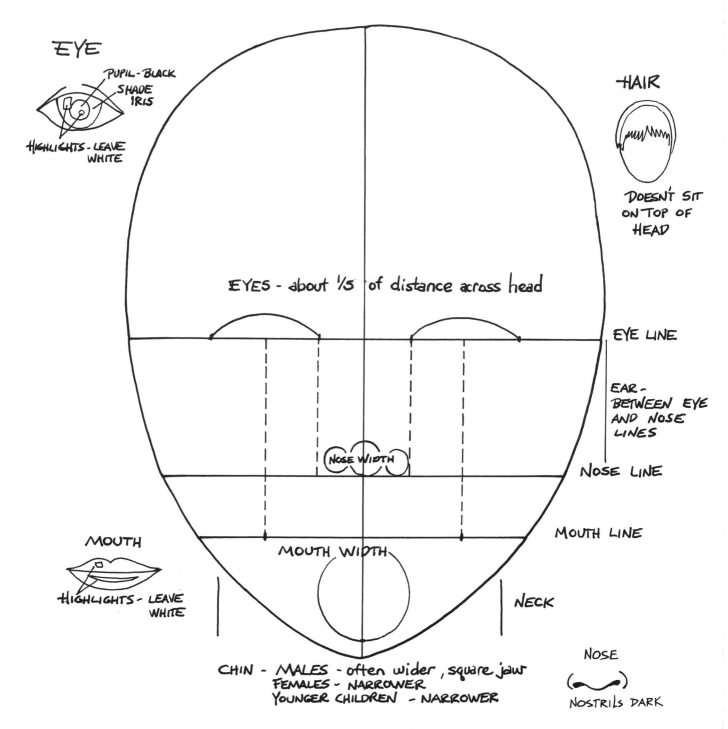

EYE

PUPIL- BLACK
SHADE
IRIS

HIGHLIGHTS - LEAVE WHITE

HAIR

DOESN'T SIT ON TOP OF HEAD

EYES - about 1/5 of distance across head

EYE LINE

EAR - BETWEEN EYE AND NOSE LINES

NOSE WIDTH

NOSE LINE

MOUTH

HIGHLIGHTS - LEAVE WHITE

MOUTH LINE

MOUTH WIDTH

NECK

CHIN - MALES - often wider, square jaw
FEMALES - NARROWER
YOUNGER CHILDREN - NARROWER

NOSE

NOSTRILS DARK

Name _____

Moving Pictures

1. Cut a piece of notebook paper to 6" x 6" square. Cut along each line to the margin line.
2. You now have a fringed piece of paper. Cut off every other strip.
3. Cut a 4" x 6" piece of cardboard, or use an index card.
4. Tape the edges of the notebook paper over the cardboard to make a frame.
5. Cut out this piece of paper and slide it into the frame you just made.

6. Draw a stick figure of a person standing with arms at the sides. Do not draw on the frame, but only on the part of the paper that shows through the frame.
7. Push the paper a little more into the frame so that the lines you just drew are completely covered by the strips of the frame.
8. On the white paper that shows through the frame, draw a stick figure again, the same size, but this time spread the legs apart and draw the arms over the head.
9. Pull the paper back and forth so you can see your drawings one after the other. Does it look like a person doing jumping jacks?
10. Use the paper as a pattern to cut out others the same size. What other moving pictures can you draw?

Name _____

Word Pictures

Each of the following represents a well-known expression. Be certain to pay careful attention to the size of the letters and their position in the box.

1. New Leaf *(upside down)*

2. THROUGH

3.  NEEDLE

4. ONESELF

5. AallLL

6. iNSULT + iNJURY *(underlined)*

7. few far and

8.  HIT

9. woWOLFol

10. g h a n *(letters arranged)*

11.  H2O H2O H2O H2O H2O H2O H2O H2O H2O H2O

12. BEND OVER *(upside down)*

13.

14. Once 3:15

214

Word Pictures II

Each of the following represents a well-known expression. Be certain to pay careful attention to the size of the letters and their position in the box.

1. READ

2. hattle = 1

3. PE rest ACE

4.

5. 1 H O L E

6.

7.

8. SKATING ICE

9.

10. ABCDEF GHIJKM NOPQRST UVWXYZ

11. ha bird nd = bu 2 sh

12. ~~GIVE~~

13. EASY ↑ HARD ↓ **find**

14. friend standing mis friend

Name _____

I.Q. Test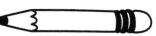

1. Please take time to read the entire test before beginning.
2. Write your name in the top right-hand corner of the paper.
3. Stand up and recite the pledge to the American flag.
4. What is a synonym for stunned? _____. Use it in a sentence. _____
5. Draw a food pyramid including the types of foods and number of servings for a healthy diet.
6. Name five European countries and their capitals. _____, _____ _____, _____, _____, _____, _____, _____, _____, _____,
7. Who were the first five presidents of the United States?_____ _____, _____, _____, _____,
8. Find the sum of 8,267.5419, 576.2, 6,478,588.993, and 23.876914. _____
9. Find the difference between 328/1,262 and 72/631. _____
10. Find the product of 8,642.2468 and 97,531.13579. _____
11. Find the quotient: 23/479 ÷ 67/536 = _____
12. Write the formula for photosynthesis. _____
13. When is it correct to say I is? _____
14. Define and give an example of each part of speech: noun, verb, adjective, adverb, pronoun, preposition, conjunction, interjection, and article. _____ _____
15. In neat cursive handwriting, write the words to "The Star-Spangled Banner," the United States' national anthem.
16. Write a paragraph about Isaac Newton and his discoveries.
17. Find the area and circumference of this circle. ⟶ ◯
18. Name an author who won the Newbery award at least two times. What are the titles of the winning books? _____
19. Define a symbiotic relationship in nature, and give an example of each of the three types.
20. Find the surface area and volume of this figure.
21. Use each circle to draw a different picture.

22. Now that you have read through the entire test, ignore questions 3-22. Do #2 and turn in your paper.

Name _____

One Hundred Words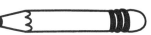

Below is a list of 100 words with which sixth grade students should be familiar. There are many things you can do with these words. You can sort them into categories, have spelling bees, use them in sentences, list them in alphabetical order. Maybe you can think of other things to do with them.

division	language	volume	perimeter
area	rounding	estimate	though
through	America	assignments	consequences
welcome	decimals	multiply	value
amazing	observe	literature	although
world	sentence	decision	newspaper
handbook	conquer	subtract	adult
planet	religion	biography	research
culture	goals	throw	common
times tables	calculator	geography	recess
chalkboard	earth	plateau	athlete
rules	heritage	process	activity
quality	product	dentist	doctor
telephone	dictionary	transportation	encyclopedia
resource	industry	article	necessary
recycle	artifact	solar system	agriculture
bicycle	landforms	separate	measurements
obvious	communicate	complete	computer
system	violence	relative	equation
quantity	discover	Internet	hemisphere
region	electricity	success	sincerely
galaxy	difference	champion	wilderness
bibliography	physical	photograph	adventure
impossible	journal	either	idea
struggle	celebrate	author	practice

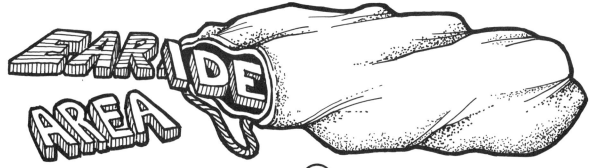

Which One?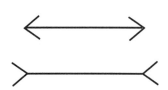

The boxes below contain optical illusions. First answer the questions by looking at the pictures. Then take out your ruler and measure.

1. Which line is longer?

2. Is the hat taller or wider?

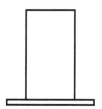

3. Which square is larger?

4. Which center circle is larger?

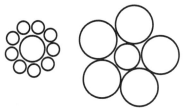

5. Which lines connect?

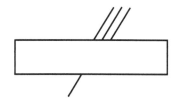

6. Which arc is longer?

7. Are you looking at two faces or a vase?

8. Which dot is closer to the center dot?

9. Are you looking at a duck or a rabbit?

10. Is the dot on the front or back of the cube?

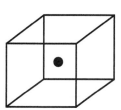

Name _____

Is It Possible?

Each box contains an optical illusion, which means that maybe you are not really seeing what you think you see. Is that possible?

1. Is the gray circle the same shade in each square?

2. Is the black on the top or bottom?

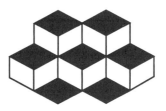

3. Is this a square with right angles?

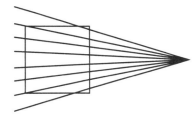

4. Is this shape physically possible

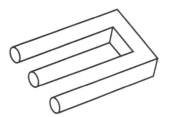

5. Is this shape physically possible?

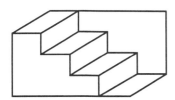

6. What's wrong here?

Where did the the cat go?

7. Are the stairs going up or down?

8. Where is the top of the stairs?

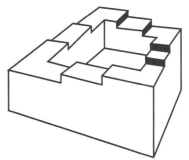

9. Do you see the spokes? How did they get there?

10. Are the dark lines parallel?

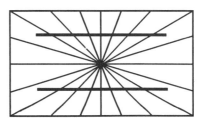

Name _____

Seeing Is Believing

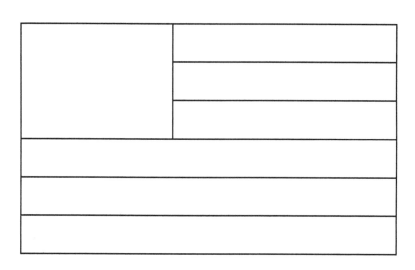

1. Color the small rectangle of the flag orange. Color the top stripe green, the next one black, and continue to alternate green, black to the bottom. You can make little black dots for stars in the orange rectangle. When you are finished, stare at the flag for thirty seconds. Then stare at a plain white piece of paper. What do you see? Do you know why that happens?

2. Color the square yellow and the circle red. Stare at it for 30 seconds and look at the blank white paper on the side. What colors do you see? _____

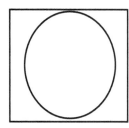 

3. What color should you color the square so that it will appear orange in the blank space after staring at it?_____ What color should you color the circle so it will appear green? _____

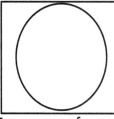 

4. Try some of your own color combinations. Can you predict what color you will see on the blank paper? _____

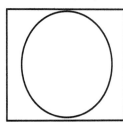 

Name _____

Mission Possible

All but one of the following is possible. Find the solution to each of them and circle the one that is not possible.

1. Connect the nine dots using only four straight lines.

2. Draw three straight lines so that each star is alone in a section of the rectangle.

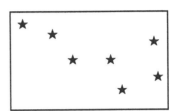

3. Draw this design without lifting your pencil from the paper or retracing over any line.

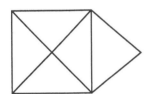

4. Draw this design without lifting your pencil from the paper or retracing over any line.

5. Draw this design without lifting your pencil from the paper or retracing over any line.

6. Draw the hopscotch game without lifting your pencil from the paper or retracing over any line.

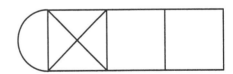

7. Draw a line connecting squares 1 and 7, another line connecting 2 and 8, a line connecting 3 and 5, and another line connecting 4 and 6. The lines cannot go out of the box or cross one another.

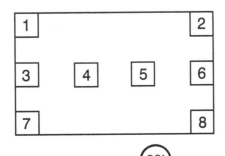

Name _____

How Well Do You Remember?

Take five minutes to look carefully at the picture below. Then, fold over the top of the paper so that you cannot see the picture any longer.

Answer the following questions according to what you remember from the picture.

1. What time was it? _____
2. How many cars were on the road? _____
3. What was the name of the street running north and south? _____
4. What season of the year was it? _____
5. How many people were in the picture? _____
6. What animals were in the picture? _____
7. Was there a fire hydrant on the corner? _____
8. What was the license number on the car at the corner? _____
9. What direction was the pickup truck headed? _____
10. Was the driver of the truck wearing glasses? _____
11. What kind of traffic signal was at the intersection? _____
12. Was there a post office in the picture? _____
13. On which street was the Gift Store? _____
14. What was the sale price of caps? _____
15. Was it a man, woman, or child sitting on the park bench? _____

Name _____

It's in the Box

Brainstorm all the different kinds of things you could do with a box.

Use this pattern to make a box. For the lid, use the same pattern.

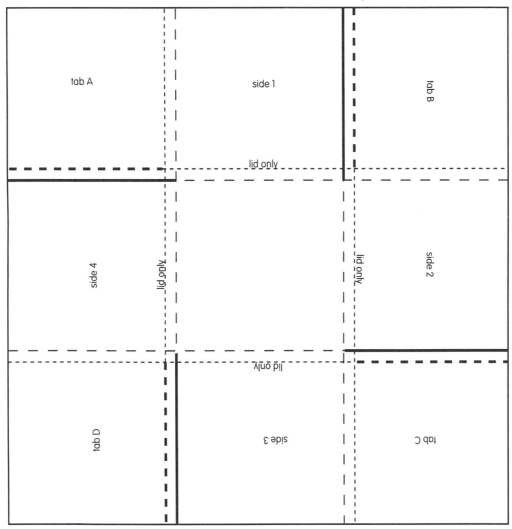

To make box:
1. Cut out square.
2. Cut on dark lines.
3. Fold in all dotted lines except those marked "lid only."
4. Attach, with tape, tab A to side 4, tab B to side 1, tab C to side 2, and tab D to side 3.

To make the lid:
1. Cut on heavy dotted lines.
2. Fold in all dotted lines marked "lid only." Then repeat step 3 from instructions above.

Use your box to play 20 questions. Put something in it and have your friends ask yes or no questions to guess what it is. Put a gift in your box to give to a favorite friend.

Name _____

Brain Teasers

Stretch your brain cells to fill in the blank with the word that shows the most accurate relationship.

1. September is to July as May is to _____. March, February, June

2. Mistake is to eraser as constitution
   is to _____. unconstitutional, amendment, bylaws

3. Yen is to Mexico as peso is to_____. pesto, Spain, Japan

4. Today is to yesterday as present is to____. tomorrow, past, now

5. Weave is to basket as throw is to _____. ball, blanket, pot

6. Conductor is to orchestra as coxswain
   is to _____. boat, train, sculling team

7. Radio is to television as silent is to ____. broadcast, talkies, movies

8. Airplane is to pilot as train is to _____. conductor, caboose, engineer

9. Beaver is to dam as eagle is to _____. sky, aerie, tree

10. Horse is to buggy as man is to _____. rickshaw, kayak, bicycle

224

Name _____

Create Your Own Food for Thought

Fill in the blanks to make your own analogies. Give them to a classmate to figure out. Make them challenging. Remember that the first two words must have the same type of relationship as the other two words. The first one has been started for you.

1. Peanut butter is to jelly as bacon is to _____.

2. _____ is to _____ as _____ is to _____.
   _____, _____, _____

3. _____ is to _____ as _____ is to _____.
   _____, _____, _____

4. _____ is to _____ as _____ is to _____.
   _____, _____, _____

5. _____ is to _____ as _____ is to _____.
   _____, _____, _____

6. _____ is to _____ as _____ is to _____.
   _____, _____, _____

7. _____ is to _____ as _____ is to _____.
   _____, _____, _____

8. _____ is to _____ as _____ is to _____.
   _____, _____, _____

Name _____

Wally's Wacky Word Processor

Wally's wacky word processor does not correct spelling errors or grammar errors. It processes a word by changing it to a number according to some rule. For example, IN: George Washington was the first president. OUT: 6 10 3 3 5 9. RULE: number of letters in each word.

Try to determine the rule Wally's wacky word processor used for each of the following sentences.

1) IN: Huckleberry Finn was written by Samuel Clemens.
   OUT: 4   1   1   2   1   3   2
   RULE:

2) IN: Victor Hugo wrote The Hunchback of Notre Dame.
   OUT: 4   2   3   2   7   1   3   2
   RULE:

3) IN: The Mississippi River borders the state of Tennessee.
   OUT: 1   1   2   2   1   2   1   1
   RULE:

4) IN: Canada is north of the United States.
   OUT: 3   1   4   1   2   3   2
   RULE:

5) IN: To be alive, Lou ate fine stew.
   OUT: 2 3   5   2   8   9   2
   RULE:

Name _____

English Sense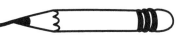

Neila, the alien from a distant galaxy, is trying to make sense of the English language. It seems that every time she applies a rule she has learned, she is wrong. Can you fill in the blanks correctly?

1. Since the plural of mouse is mice, Neila thought the plural of _____ would be hice instead of _____.

2. Since the plural of foot is feet, Neila thought the plural of _____ would be beet instead of_____.

3. Since the plural of ox is oxen, Neila thought the plural of _____ would be boxen instead of _____.

4. Since the past tense of fly is flew, Neila thought the past tense of _____ would be applew instead of _____.

5. Since the past tense of lead is led, Neila thought the past tense of _____ would be red instead of _____.

6. Since the past tense of see is saw, Neila thought the past tense of_____ would be fraw instead of _____.

Certificate
of
Outstanding Achievement

Awarded to

_____

for going above and beyond expectations in

_____

_____   _____
Date   Signature

KINDNESS AWARD

It is hereby announced that

_____

has been caught doing this extra kind deed

_____

and is awarded
this certificate of appreciation

this_____day of_____,_____

_____   _____
Witness   Witness

Answer Key

What Are Decimals Doing in the Library? page 13
1. 400s
2. 200s
3. 700s
4. 900s
5. 500s
6. 600s
7. 900s
8. 700s
9. 500s
10. 800s

Library Scavenger Hunt page 14
1. **Sign of The Beaver, Bronze Bow, Witch of Blackbird Pond**
2. Answers will vary.
3. Number in the 600s
4. Paul Gob
5. Category to find it. Author's last name.
6. Answers will vary.
7. Answers will vary.
8. Answers will vary.
9. 780s
10. Answers will vary.

To Do or Not to Do, That Is the Question page 18
1. cons
2. There are more reasons not to do it.

Memory Techniques page 20
1. cow

More Memory Techniques page 21
to remember the color spectrum: Roy G. Biv (red, orange, yellow, green, blue, indigo, and violet)

Sarah Sees Seven Seashells page 22
1. swum
2. went
3. worn
4. ate, eats
5. chosen
6. broke
7. shrunk
8. blew
9. fallen
10. brought
11. came
12. sank
13. known
14. drink
15. ran, runs
16. ridden
17. begun
18. froze
19. done
20. saw

Mackinac Island page 23
Mackinac Island is a three-mile-long and two-mile-wide island that <u>sits</u> in the Straits of Mackinac, the water that separates Michigan's Upper and Lower peninsulas. Lake Huron <u>lies</u> to the east of the island. French explorers <u>set</u> foot on Mackinac Island first in the 1600s. It was an ancient Indian burial ground called Mishilimackinas by the Chippewas, meaning "great turtle" or "great spirit." The British later raised a fort there. After the United States <u>laid</u> claim to the island, John Jacob Aster <u>set</u> up a fur company.

Today Mackinac Island is a popular summer resort. Jet boats whisk tourists from Mackinaw City and St. Ignace to Mackinac Island. When you <u>set</u> foot on the island dock, you may feel as though you are in the eighteenth or nineteenth century. First of all, you will see horses and wagons going up and down the streets. There are no cars. Motor vehicles were banned in the late 1800s, so the only transportation is horse and wagon or bicycle.

As you <u>rise</u> early the next morning after your arrival, you may decide to tour the island. The first thing you see is someone raising the flag. Shops are beginning to open. Your favorite may be the fudge shop where 30-pound slabs of fudge are <u>sitting</u> on the counter to tempt you. Everything from antiques to T-shirts is available. As you roam the island, you cannot miss the century-old Grand Hotel which <u>sits</u> on a hill above the village. It is a showplace with its 700-foot-long porch, yellow awnings, and American flags rippling in the breeze. White rocking chairs line the porch along with potted red geraniums. If you would like to <u>sit</u> on this porch and watch the sun <u>rise</u> or set, just pay about $250 per night and you may.

Pick a Pronoun page 24
The following words should be circled:
1. he
2. she
3. him
4. I
5. they
6. me
7. us
8. me
9. We
10. her

1. I
2. We
3. him
4. he/she
5. them
6. they
7. me
8. we, her, us
9. you, me

Little Lottie Litchfield page 25
1. larger, largest
2. more cheerful, most cheerful
3. better, best
4. swifter, swiftest
5. more frequent, most frequent
6. worse, worst
7. fancier, fanciest
8. healthier, healthiest
9. more current, most current
10. more pleasant, most pleasant

1. sadder
2. heaviest
3. more difficult
4. more amazing
5. most careful
6. cuter
7. funniest
8. more intelligent
9. shortest
10. more daring

When Where, and How? page 26
1. hurriedly, 3
2. here, anxiously, 2, 3
3. Fearfully, 3
4. Yesterday, well, 1, 3
5. now, 1
6. down, abruptly, 2, 3
7. Then, brilliantly, down, 1, 3, 2
8. deeply, suddenly, there, 3, 3, 2
9. incredulously, soon, 3, 1
10. Then, lightly, faithfully, 1, 3, 3

1-14. Answers will vary.

Across the Page page 27
1. on
2. towards
3. in
4. up
5. out
6. down
7. under
8. between
9. over
10. around
11. across
12. through
13. to

The Conjunction Connection page 28
1. before
2. until
3. and
4. when
5. whether, or
6. When
7. because
8. but
9. while
10. although
1-6. Answers will vary.

Oh, Yeah! page 29
1. Ouch!
2. Yippee!
3. Oh, yuck!
4. Goodness, gracious!
5. Hooray!
6. Hey!
7. Ugh!
8. Hallelujah!
9. Hello!
10. Good grief!
1.-10. Answers will vary.

"Object"ively Speaking page 30
1. grocery
2. lemonade
3. dogs, cows
4. living room
5. oats
6. novel
7. head
8. nickel
9. roses
10. tourist

1. doughnut (me)
2. tale (Teddy)
3. dollars (myself)
4. hamburger (Horace)
5. football (Sally)
6. photograph (aunt)
7. bucket (Valerie)
8. crickets (Kendra)
9. bits (piranha)
10. trip (Gary)

The Wastebasket
page 32

Just the other day the teacher asked Tim, "Will you empty the wastebasket and then lead the class in the pledge to the flag?"

Tim said, "Yes." However, when he went to empty the wastebasket, it ran away from him. He and the teacher went running down the hall, chasing the wastebasket. "Oh, no!" Tim cried. "It's going into the principal's office!" The principal was holding an important meeting and was startled by the intrusion of Tim, his teacher, and the wastebasket.

"What is going on here?" the principal shouted. "Tim, why are you chasing the wastebasket and, Mrs. Jones, why are you out of your classroom? What is this ridiculous wastebasket doing in my office?" Tim felt awful and could not say a word.

Mrs. Jones told him, "Go back to the classroom and begin the pledge to the flag. I'll be there shortly."

So Tim hurried back to the classroom and had all the students stand. He started to lead the pledge: "I pledge allegiance to the flag . . . ." When he began to say the pledge, the flag rolled up. When he stopped reciting the pledge, the flag unrolled. Of course, all the students started giggling. Tim could not understand what was going on and thought someone was playing a joke on him. "Okay, what's going on here?" he asked. "Who's the wise guy?" He had already been in trouble once and did not want to get in trouble twice in the same day.

Mrs. Jones had heard the laughter and raced back to the classroom to quiet the class. "Quiet!" she yelled. "You are disturbing all the classes." When she saw why the students were all laughing, she burst into laughter too.

By this time the principal heard the laughter and stormed toward the uproar. As he neared the classroom door, he shouted, "If you do not stop laughing, you will all stay after school!" But no one could hear him because they were all laughing so hard; and when he saw what was happening, he started laughing along with the rest. Soon all the students in the school had crowded into or near the classroom, and everyone joined in the laughter.

Add the Apostrophes
page 33

1. mother's
2. Didn't, boys'
3. couldn't, Frank's
4. bird's (or birds'), wind's
5. it's
6. You're, teacher's, Betsy's
7. Where've
8. cousin's (or cousins'), isn't
9. won't, Patty's
10. we're, Grandma's
11. we'd, he'd, would've, Bert's
12. child's, uncle's, newspapers'
13. Seth's, Nate's, he'd
14. wrestlers', Matt's

1. isn't
2. couldn't
3. shan't
4. let's
5. he's
6. we're
7. here's
8. won't
9. hasn't
10. she'll

Hmm, What Do I Need?
page 34

1. 7:15
2. calf;
3. large, boisterous, us,
4. band;
5. Madame:
6. panel: Peter, Jeremy, Tara,
7. 4:00, work; 6:00
8. Steve, following: soufflé, spaghetti, sherbet,
9. Leah, Dave; 8;30
10. made: sweaters, canes, toothpicks, pens,
11. us;
12. Joe, you,
13. 2:10 P.M., 3:05
14. open;
15. concern: zoo, farm,
16. sea;

What Is It?
page 35

1. ! exclamation
2. ? question
3. . statement
4. . command
5. ? question
6. ! exclamation
7. . statement
8. . statement
9. ? question
10. ! exclamation
11. . command
12. ? question
13. . statement
14. . statement
15. ? question
16. . statement
17. . command
18. ! exclamation
19. . command
20. . statement

A Troubling Tale
page 36

1. liked
2. packed, placed
3. skipped
4. was
5. cried, are
6. am, is, replied
7. pay, mewed
8. scampered, dawdled
9. thrust, disguised, plopped
10. knocked, is
11. squeaked, come, visit
12. stepped, stopped

The Electric Impact
page 37

There are some advantages of having an electric car. General Motors' Impact is a good example. It has power, goes from a standstill to 60 mph instantly, and handles well on the road. The dashboard in the Impact gives a wealth of information. In addition to telling the speed, it shows how far you can go before recharging. If you happen to forget that the car is plugged into an electric socket, there is a warning light. Also the words "check messages" flash when the warning lights go on somewhere else. The dashboard will also tell the driver of any motor or battery problems, if there is a low tire, or if the road is slick.

Doesn't all this sound wonderful? Well, it is. However, one big problem is that if you run out of juice, you cannot stop at someone's house and plug the car into an outlet for a short time and then go on your way. It takes 3 to 12 hours to charge the battery. There's the possibility that you may forget to plug in the car overnight. In that case you may have to find another way to get to work or to school the next morning.

What's the Point?
page 38

1. Stephanie didn't know what to do.
2. This was the lousiest day of my life.
3. Sometimes you need a cold drink to keep you going.
4. Ben loved camping.
5. What our school needs is a swimming pool.

Walt Disney
page 39

Walt Disney once said, "Like most people, I have fun just watching others have fun." Many of you have probably visited Disneyland, an amusement park in Anaheim, California, or Disney World near Orlando, Florida. I'm sure you're familiar with characters like Mickey Mouse and Donald Duck, but do you know much about the person responsible for these places and characters? Many years ago before you were even born, Walt Disney began creating cartoon film characters. Then he produced full-length cartoon movies and movies about wild animals.

Walt Disney was born in Chicago, Illinois, in 1901. When he was a child, his family moved from Chicago to Missouri. He spent much of his boyhood on a farm near Marceline where he acquired a love for animals. He later studied art in Chicago at the age of 18, but in his early twenties he moved to Los Angeles, California. Walt worked hard for a few years just making enough to pay his bills. Then Mickey Mouse saved him! Walt's first short Mickey Mouse film was a hit. This led to more cartoons with characters like Donald Duck, Goofy, and Pluto and finally to movies such as **Snow White and the Seven Dwarfs, Bambi, Cinderella**, and **Lady and the Tramp**.

Probably Walt Disney's greatest success came when he opened Disneyland, an amusement park unlike any other park. At the time he was ridiculed by other amusement park owners. They told him, "You will never succeed with this idea. This is just like all the other amusement parks." Walt proved them wrong. He planned a similar park, Walt Disney World in Florida. It was completed in 1971 after his death in 1966. It continues to be a very popular vacation spot for children and adults. Why was Walt Disney so successful? It was probably because of hard work, practical knowledge, and foresight. Maybe there's a lesson here for all of us.

Silence Is Golden
page 41

1. answer
2. gnat
3. stalk
4. glisten
5. limb
6. might
7. valet
8. witch
9. honor
10. Sioux
11. would
12. bridge
13. reign
14. physique
15. whistle
16. ought
17. wreath
18. tomb
19. sword
20. sign
21. written
22. patch
23. silhouette
24. Chevrolet
25. though
26. bologna
27. psychic
28. rhyme
29. Wednesday
30. cologne
31. leopard
32. Illinois
33. calf
34. knit
35. hour
36. buffet
37. rhubarb
38. honest
39. fought
40. psalm
41. gourmet
42. campaign
43. Arkansas
44. wedge
45. beret
46. two
47. should
48. castle
49. rhombus
50. unique
51. ledge
52. pterodactyl
53. watch
54. gnome

You're a Pro!
page 42

A = 2 B = 7 C = 18 D = 12
E = 8 F = 5 G = 11 H = 15
I = 13 J = 17 K = 6 L = 3
M = 16 N = 10 O = 4 P = 9

1. probe   2. proportion
1. probe   4. promise
2. project   5. progress
3. produce   6. proportion
magic square sum = 39

Classified Ads
page 43

Noun
1. adventure
2. advantage
3. adjective
4. address
5. advance
6. adult
7. advent
8. advice

Verb
1. advise
2. adopt
3. admire
4. address
5. admit
6. advance
7. admonish
8. adapt
9. adhere
10. adjust
11. adorn

Adjective
1. adequate
2. advance
3. adult

Arithmetician/Magician
page 44

1. Phoenician's
2. mortician's
3. diagnostician's
4. physician's
5. beautician's
6. optician's
7. mathematician's
8. statistician's
9. arithmetician's
10. theoretician's
11. musician's
12. magician's
13. clinician's
14. electrician's
15. obstetrician's
16. politician's
17. dietician's
18. technician's
The word is Phoenician.

Fractured Compounds
page 45

1. road
2. lady
3. air
4. rose
5. arch
6. key
7. bob
8. pull
9. free
10. mill
11. pay
12. green
13. counter
14. off
15. dead
16. egg
17. ring
18. back
19. bed

Long Form
page 46

What's It All About?
page 47

1. l
2. f
3. j
4. h
5. d
6. n
7. g
8. k
9. c
10. i
11. o
12. e
13. a
14. b
15. m

Opposing Views
page 48

1. m
2. a
3. j
4. t
5. p
6. d
7. f
8. w
9. q
10. v
11. b
12. l
13. h
14. s
15. g
16. x
17. n
18. c
19. k
20. i
21. e
22. r
23. o
24. u

A Page for a Sage
page 50

1. nose hose
2. trick stick
3. duck truck
4. mouse house
5. deer fear
6. far star
7. fruit newt
8. toad road
9. socks box
10. loose goose

1. yellow jello
2. fender bender
3. rocket socket
4. turtle hurdle
5. mutton glutton
6. willow pillow
7. certain curtain
8. soccer locker
9. table label
10. flower tower

1. reservation preservation
2. commuter computer

As Alike as Two Peas in a Pod
page 51

Answers will vary.

Sing Is to Song, as . . . .
page 54

1. writing
2. father
3. state
4. 12
5. books
6. ocean
7. ice
8. bad
9. scales
10. tricycle
11. canoe
12. dance
13. wait
14. French
15. hospital
16. Japan
17. honk or baa
18. pack
19. golf

Who's the Real Bad Guy?
page 62

1. Jack's
2. Red Riding Hood's
3. the bears'
4. the pigs'
5. Cinderella's
6. the goats'

Fair Share
page 71

1. 30
2. 5
3. 8
4. 12, 180
5. 5
6. 180, 360
7. pig - 270, chihuahua - 202.5, goat - 67.5 pig
Extension: 13 weeks

Monkey in the Middle
page 72

1. 1/3
2. 6/10
3. 4/8
4. 2/6
5. 3/10
6. 5/8
7. 8/12
8. 1/2
9. 5/6
10. 7/10
11. 3/8
12. 7/14
13. 3/6
14. 5/8
15. 2/3
16. 4/6
17. 5/7
18. 1/3
19. 2/5
20. 4/5

Doing Decimals
page 73

1. 38.4
2. 36.28
3. 74.7
4. 5.53
5. 189.68
6. 32.37
7. 1.26
8. 77.15

9. 8.17
10. .71
11. 90.12
12. 76.65
13. 1.25
14. 37.26
15. 183.88
16. 249.91
17. 5.7
18. 142.62
19. 148.58
20. 55.69
21. 0.048
22. 48.128
23. 2.65

"The Eagle has Landed." - Apollo

Shopping for Soccer Supplies
page 74

1. Sports Corner, $.32
2. Joe's Soccer, $.98
3. $31.47, $27.22
4. Joe's Soccer, $2.97
5. Sports Center, $.30

Extension: $825.55

Patterns Plus
page 75

1. 27, 33, 39 Add 6.
2. 900, 504, 405, 306 Subtract 99.
3. 40, 48, 56, 64 Add 8.
4. 91, 55, 46, 37 Subtract 9.
5. 20, 27, 35 Add 3, then 4, then 5, etc.
6. 506, 607, 708, 809 Add 101.
7. 90, 80, 75, 65 Subtract 5.
8. 28, 40, 52, 58 Add 6.
9. 2, 4, 32, 128 Multiply by 2.
10. 44, 52, 68, 76 Add 8.
11. 44, 49, 53 Add 9 to first number, 8 to next, then 7, etc.
12. 34, 66,130 Add 2, then add by multiples of 2.

Money Matters
page 76

1. 2, 4, 6, 8, 10, 12
2. 3, 5, 7, 9, 11, 13
3. 2, 4, 6, 8, 10, 12, 14
   6, 5, 4, 3, 2, 1, 0
4. 3, 5, 7, 9, 11, 13, 15
   6, 5, 4, 3, 2, 1, 0
5. 3, 5, 7, 9, 11, 13, 15, 17, 19
   8, 7, 6, 5, 4, 3, 2, 1, 0
6. 3, 5, 7, 9, 11, 13, 15, 17, 19, 21, 23, 25
   7, 6, 5, 4, 3, 2, 1, 0

```
#5   4  6  8  10 12 14  16 18 20
#10  8  7  6  5  4  3   2  1  0
#20  0  0  0  0  0  0   0  0  0
```

```
$ 5- 0 0 2 4 0 2 4 6 8 0 2 4 6 8 10 12 0 2 4 6 8 10 12 14 16 0 2
$10- 0 2 1 0 4 3 2 1 0 6 5 4 3 2 1 0 8 7 6 5 4 3 2 1 0 10 9
$20-5 4 4 4 3 3 3 3 2 2 2 2 2 2 1 1 1 1 1 1 1 1 0 0
```

All Primed Up
page 77

Because he was off base.

Percent Pro
page 78

1. 320
2. 8.8
3. 42
4. 408
5. 14.5
6. 1.8
7. 100
8. 80
9. 11.4
10. 105
11. 126
12. 16
13. 67.5
14. 67.6
15. 2.8
16. 4
17. 34
18. 247.5
19. 0.6
20. 57

Lazlo Biro

Savemore National Bank
page 79

1. .99, 13.34
2. 2.08, 21.01
3. 10.28, 11.38, 12.48
4. 66.42
5. 22.94, 112.89

Paper Drive
page 80

1. 85
2. 86, yes, $1.00
3. 87, $1.00, $2.00
4. $86
5. $66
6. No, they tied. 66
7. $73

Extension: 77.17 per group

School Property Dimensions
page 81

1. 492 ft.
2. 12,104 sq. ft.
3. 70 sq. ft.
4. 48 sq. ft.
5. $9,504
6. 2,982 ft.
7. 542,198 sq. ft.
8. 530,094 sq. ft.
9. 944,112 cu. ft.

Choko Airlines . . . Dogtown Airport
page 82

1. 3 hrs., 2 min.
2. 28 min.
3. 2:04 p.m.
4. 2 hr. 52 min.
5. 6 hrs.. 15 min.
6. 1 hr. 43 min.
7. 1 hr. 20 min.
8. 30 min.
9. 11:20 a.m.

Calculate This!
page 83

1. chips ($.31), chili dog ($.85)
   2 medium colas ($1.48), Burger Princess Supreme ($1.48)
2. a. 9,876,543 - 1 = 9,876,542
   b. 5,123 - 4,987 = 136
   c. 9,876,543 + 2 = 9,876545
   d. 1,357 + 2,468 = 3,825
   e. 9,642 x 8,753 = 84,396,426
   f. 2,345,678 x 1 = 2,345,678
   g. 9,876,543 ÷ 1 = 9, 876,543
   h. 6,123 ÷ 5987 = 1.0227168
3. 60¢

Do As the Romans Do
page 84

23 = XXIII
44 = XLIV
52 = LII
17 = XVII
68 = LXVIII
99 = XCIX
1,111 = MCXI
575 = DLXXV
946 = CMXLVI

1. XL
2. XXV
3. DCCC
4. XLII
5. LXVI
6. L
7. V
8. XV
9. LXXXIII
10. MLXIII
11. CCCXXXV
12. LXXX
13. LXXV
14. CCXL
15. XL
16. VI

17. Accept reasonable answers. It takes a lot of digits to write a number.

Weather Graphing
page 85

1. Average Number of Rainy Days in Miami, Florida
2. Rainy Days
3. Names of Months
4. September
5. Oct.-Nov.
6. Feb.
7. Feb. and Nov. They were the driest.
8. 20
9. 12.04
10. 8.75
11. 7.5

Compiling Data
page 86

1993 State Populations

Income per Capita

Heights of Garden Flowers

IF8679 A Little Bit of Everything

Compiling Data II   page 87

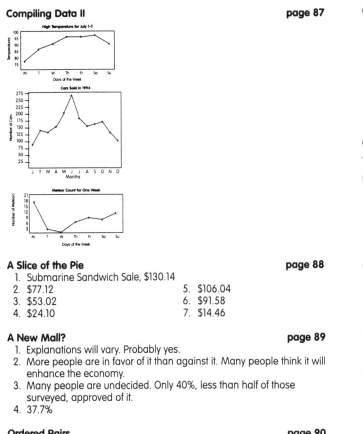

A Slice of the Pie   page 88
1. Submarine Sandwich Sale, $130.14
2. $77.12
3. $53.02
4. $24.10
5. $106.04
6. $91.58
7. $14.46

A New Mall?   page 89
1. Explanations will vary. Probably yes.
2. More people are in favor of it than against it. Many people think it will enhance the economy.
3. Many people are undecided. Only 40%, less than half of those surveyed, approved of it.
4. 37.7%

Ordered Pairs   page 90
1. The Letter M
2. Paper towel
3. Sixty

Freezing Temperatures   page 91
1. -1°
2. 23°
3. -9°
4. 42°
5. 32°

How Much Is a Liter?   page 92
Answers will vary.

Time Can Mean So Much!   page 93
1. 47.25
2. 66.15
3. 28.35
4. 85.05

1. 3, 28.35
2. 7, 66.15
3. 4, 37.80
4. 9, 85.05

1. 3
2. 5
3. 6
4. 9

Have You Ever Been on "Metric Road"?   page 94

Calculator Calculations   page 95
1. 5
2. 9
3. 17
4. 4
5. 10
6. 7
7. 15
8. 12
9. 20
10. 41
11. 25
12. 13
13. 2
14. 1
15. 36
16. 81
17. 23
18. 26

Challenges to Amaze You!   page 96
Answers will vary.

Here's a Challenge for You!   page 97
1. 4, 1
2. 4
3. yes, 18
4. 7
5. more, 20 cm

Area of Art   page 99
A. 78.5
B. 48
C. 30
D. 10
E. 25

A. 113.04
B. 69.12
C. 43.2
D. 14.4
E. 36

Total Area: 191.5 sq. ft.   Total Area: 275.76
No. Accept reasonable explanations.

Street Sense   page 100
1. 4th, 7th, 8th
   Front, Dublin, Scioto, Best, Broad, or Park
2. 8th, 7th, 5th, Broad, 4th
3. perpendicular
4. intersect
5. Dublin Road
6. Scioto Road
7. Front and 7th
8. Best, Broad, and Park

How Much Will It Cost?   page 101

Income	Expenses	
10.00	save	2.50
16.00	donate	2.50
26.00	shirt	7.00
	movies	3.00
	concessions	3.00
	present	5.00
	book	4.00
	gum and candy	3.00
	souvenir	2.00
deficit = $6.00		$32.00

1. earn more money
2. spend less

Number Wise   page 103
1. 14
2. 50
3. 5,280
4. 10
5. 32°
6. 12
7. 3
8. 1776
9. 16
10. 0
11. 100
12. 7
13. 144
14. 4
15. 1,000
16. 8
17. 24
18. 5
19. 6
20. 365

Mixed-Up Measures   page 104
1. acre — area
2. kilometer — length
3. liter — volume
4. league — distance
5. second — time
6. gallon — volume
7. ampere — electrical current
8. furlong — length
9. carat — weight

10. kilogram — mass
11. cubit — length
12. horsepower — power
13. decibel — relative loudness
14. degree — temperature
15. hectare — area
16. fathom — length
17. teaspoon — volume
18. bushel — volume

Nine Square Dare — page 105

1	7	4	8	6	3	2	9	5
2	8	3	5	7	9	6	1	4
6	9	5	2	4	1	3	7	8
3	1	7	4	5	8	9	6	2
4	5	2	7	9	6	8	3	1
8	6	9	3	1	2	5	4	7
9	4	6	1	2	5	7	8	3
5	3	1	9	8	7	4	2	6
7	2	8	6	3	4	1	5	9

Math Maze — page 106

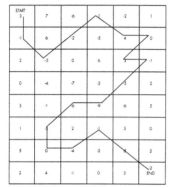

Valentine Exchange — page 107

Using clue E, you can see that Esther must have received #5 from Ivan. Thus, Danielle, who could have received either #3 or #5, must have received #3. Likewise, Bethany must have been sent #2, Chelsea #4, and Abigail #1.

Dinner Winner — page 108

Combine clues 1 and 5 to place Mr. and Mrs. Top correctly. Next, go to clue 7 to place Mr. Bottom and Mrs. Left. Clue 6 allows the placement of Mrs. Bottom across from her husband. Then use clue 3 to place Mr. Left and clue 4 to place Mrs. Right. Clue 2 allows the placement of Mr. Center. Going back to clue 6, see that Mr. Right cannot sit in the empty seat across from his wife, so he must be placed in the seat next to her. That leaves Mrs. Center to fill the empty chair in the top corner.
Diagram:

	Mrs. Center	Mr. Left	Mr. Center	Mrs. Bottom	
Mr. Top					Mrs. Top
	Mrs. Right	Mr. Right	Mrs. Left	Mr. Bottom	

An Average Class — page 109

1. 6
2. 5
3. Any outcome with a total of 60 letters will work. Here is one possible solution:
   Joel Johnson   Jerry Richards
   James Ballard   Joshua Fisher
   Janet Griffin
4. Again there are many possibilities. Here is one that uses ten names, four of which have exactly three letters:
   Lee   Ann   Amy   Joy   Ed
   Al   Jo   Carl   Mark   Gary
5. Here is one possible solution that uses ten names (many from an Irish phone book), two of which have exactly ten letters:
   Cairnduff   MacPherson   Milligan   VanOverbeke
   O'Callaghan   Crawford   Fairbrother   Armstrong
   Tullybrannigan Weatherhead

Dated Odds — page 110

A. 1/30
B. 4/30 = 2/15
C. 5/30 = 1/6
D. 21/30 = 7/10
E. 9/30 = 3/10
F. 15/30 = 1/2
G. 12/30 = 2/15
H. 12/30 = 2/5
I. 21/30 = 7/10
J. 2/30 = 1/15
K. 0/30 = 0
L. 21/30 = 7/10

Paint Point — page 111

1.
2. Impossible
3.
4.
5.
6. Impossible

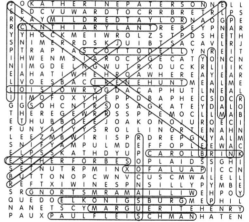

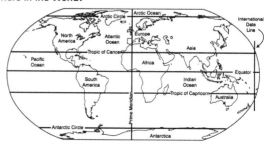

What's My Number? — page 112

1. 336
2. 551
3. 144
4. 4,567
5. 6,666
6. 7
7. 22
8. 135

Authors — page 123

They have all won the Newbery Award.

Scavenger Hunt — page 124

1. 30 m.p.h.
2. Kaline
3. Dr. Nipsy
4. Terrace Boulevard
5. avocado
6. August 11-15
7. a candidate for school board
8. penny loafers
9. if you love Elvis
10. Federal Bank

Folklore Newspaper — page 125

Answers will vary.

Where in the World? — page 127

Map Review

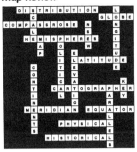

page 128

Out of Africa

page 129

African Scavenger Hunt

page 130

1. 3°S 37°E
2. 12°N 43°E
3. 16°N 33°E
4. 30°N 31°E
5. 7°N 3°E
6. 4°S 15°E
7. 23°N 32°E
8. 2°N 20°E
9. 12°N 4°E
10. 24°N 10°E
11. 23°S 22°E
12. 22°S 14°E
13. 1°S 33°E
14. 6°S 30°E
15. 34°S 19°E
16. 34°S 20°E
17. 18°S 25°E
18. 2°S 35°E
19. 3°S 35°E
20. 17°N 2°W
21. 23°S 14°E
22. 6°S 21°E
23. 34°S 21°E

Relative Location in Africa

page 131

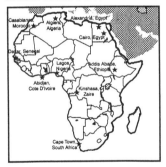

Coming to America

page 132

North American Scramble

page 133

1. Mexico
2. Superior
3. Greenland
4. Barbados
5. Niagara
6. McKinley
7. Waialeale
8. Bermuda
9. Bahamas
10. Panama
11. Canada
12. Antilles
13. Death Valley
14. Sequoia
15. Columbia
16. Aleutian
17. United States
18. Rio Grande
19. Rocky
20. Redwood

Climograph

page 134

1. drier than summer
2. wetter than winter
3. yes
4. yes
5. no
6. yes
7. either
8. no
9. yes
10. yes

11. Oklahoma City, Oklahoma; Dallas, Texas; San Antonio, Texas; Houston, Texas; New Orleans, Louisiana; Baton Rouge, Louisiana; Little Rock, Arkansas; Louisville, Kentucky; Nashville, Tennessee; Birmingham, Alabama; Richmond, Virginia; Raleigh, North Carolina; Columbia, South Carolina; Charleston, South Carolina; Atlanta, Georgia; Tallahassee, Florida; Orlando, Florida; Jackson, Mississippi

All Around Asia

page 135

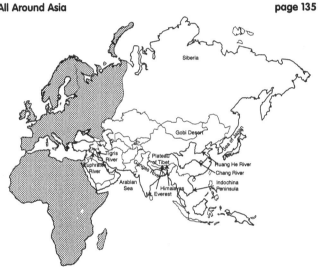

Asia

page 136

1. 8°S 111°E
2. 1°N 103°E
3. 5°N 114°E
4. 13°N 102°E
5. 23°N 90°E
6. 28°N 86°E
7. 18°N 72°E
8. 34°N 71°E
9. 29°N 33°E
10. 31°N 35°E
11. 41°N 29°E
12. 40°N 52°E
13. 81°N 40°E
14. 35°N 139°E
15. 37°N 127°E
16. 45°N 126°E
17. 39°N 116°E
18. 31°N 121°E
19. 21°N 115°E

What Is My Name?

page 137

1. Caspian Sea
2. South China Sea
3. Dead Sea
4. Arabian Peninsula
5. Lake Baikal
6. Bay of Bengal
7. Indonesia
8. Red Sea
9. Yellow River and Yellow Sea
10. Ob River

Exploring Europe
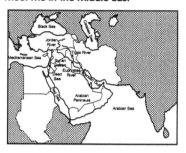

page 138

Absolute Location in Europe
page 139

1. 51° N 0°
2. 41° N 12° E
3. 60° N 24° E
4. 55° N 37° E
5. 51° N 51° E
6. Answers will vary.
7. 11:00 P.M.
8. 2:00 P.M.
9. 64° N 21° E
10. 53° N 6° W
11. 38° N 9° W
12. 40° N 3° W
13. 5:00 A.M.
14. 6:00 A.M.
15. the same, Wednesday
16. nothing, it is still the same
17. Thursday
18. traveling west across seven time zones and not crossing the International Date Line
19. traveling west crossing the International Date Line, add a day
20. in a great-circle route over the Arctic Ocean
21. Answers will vary.
    Possibilities: to be able to conduct international business and to estimate times
22. Answers will vary.
    Possibilities: to be able to conserve aviation fuel, which is quite expensive, to be able to take the shortest amount of time when traveling

Relative Location in Europe
page 140

1. Scandinavian, North
2. Jutland, North
3. Mediterranean, Pyrenees, Iberian
4. Italian, Mediterranean, Tyrrhenian
5. Italy, Rome
6. Balkan, Ionian, Aegean
7. southern, Crete
8. Hungary, Switzerland, Moldova, Macedonia
9. Spain, Mediterranean
10. British, Scotland
11. Northern Ireland, Irish
12. Ural, Europe, Caspian, Black

S.W.O.T. Team
page 141

1. W
2. S
3. W
4. W
5. O
6. O
7. O
8. W
9. T
10. S
11. O
12. T
13. T
14. S
15. O
16. T
17. W
18. O
19. W

Relative Location in the CIS
page 142

1. Armenia
2. approximately 4,845,688 square miles
3. Russia and Kazakhstan
4. Tajikistan
5. Russia
6. Russia
7. Russia, Kazakhstan, Turkmenistan, and Azerbaijan
8. Armenia, Kyrgyzstan, Tajikistan, Turkmenistan, and Uzbekistan (Belarus, Moldova, and Ukraine are completely in Europe.)
9. Caucasus Mountains

Meet Me in the Middle East
page 143

Relative Location in North Africa/Middle East
page 144

1. Turkey
2. Egypt
3. Israel
4. Saudi Arabia
5. Bahrain
6. Morocco
7. Afghanistan

Oceania
page 145

```
C O R A L            C O C O N U T
    1                10     11
F A U N A            F I S H I N G
  2                        12
F L O R A            L A G O O N S
  3                    13
G U A N O            O C E A N I A
4                            14
R E E F S            D R O U G H T S
    5                15      16
W A T E R            M O U N T A I N
6                          17
W I N D S            R A I N F A L L
  7                      18
A T O L L S          V O L C A N I C
    8                      19
F O R E S T          S U B S I S T E N C E
  9                  20      21
H I G H   I S L A N D S     L O W   I S L A N D S
12 14 4 16  18 21 8 1 19 15 5   3 10 6  17 9 13 2 11 7 20
```

World Records
page 146

1. North America
2. Asia
3. Andes
4. Nile
5. South Africa
6. Caspian Sea
7. Patagonia
8. Greenland
9. Himalayas
10. Great Wall of China
11. Amazon
12. Asia
13. Dead Sea
14. Fertile Crescent

A River Runs Through It
page 147

1. Euphrates River
2. Pyramids
3. Rosetta Stone
4. 4,000+ miles
5. cubit
6. Sirius
7. Milky Way
8. Osiris
9. Delta
10. White and Blue
11. cataracts
12. Aswan Dam

Hieroglyphics
page 148

What do you call a giant mummy? gauzilla

Seven Wonders of the Ancient World page 149

What's in a Name? page 151

1. I	11. C
2. L	12. R
3. D	13. A
4. Q	14. K
5. G	15. O
6. N	16. F
7. S	17. M
8. J	18. H
9. B	19. T
10. P	20. E

Real Renaissance People page 152

1. f	8. d
2. c	9. l
3. e	10. g
4. n	11. i
5. j	12. m
6. h	13. a
7. o	14. b
	15. k

Can You Dig It? page 153

1B - pot with designs, wide at bottom, narrow neck, to carry water
1E - moccasin with fringes made of animal skin, shoe, footwear
3A, 2B, 1C - arrow—sharp point, stick, feathers, for hunting food
2D - 2E basket woven from reeds, for carrying things
2E - 2F - plate or bowl, for eating or holding food
3B, C, D, E - hoe, for cooking, working in the garden

Religions page 155

Religion	symbol	holy book	leader	where it originated
Buddhism	Buddha Statue	Buddhist texts Four Noble Truths	Siddhartha Gautama Buddha	Near the Himalaya Mountains
Hinduism		Vedas	Vishnu Shiva Devi Krishna	Aryans-India
Confucianism		Analects of Confucius	Confucius	China
Islam (also called Muslims)		Koran	Muhammad	Mecca, Arabia
Judaism	Star of David	Torah	Abraham	Canaan (Israel)
Christianity	Cross	Bible	Jesus Christ	Israel

Historical Time Line page 156

1. 5000 years
2. Etruscans settle in Italy
3. Chinese invented paper
4. King Solomon, Etruscans, Toltec people in Mexico

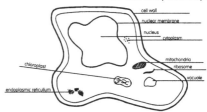

© Instructional Fair • TS Denison

Who Said That? page 158

1. All roads lead to Rome.
2. When in Rome, do as the Romans do.
3. It's all Greek to me.
4. She met her Waterloo.
5. Et tu, Brute?
6. Montezuma's revenge

Building Blocks of Plants page 162

1. cell wall	5. nucleus
2. ribosome	6. cytoplasm
3. chloroplast	7. mitochondria
4. endoplasmic reticulum	8. vacuole
	9. nuclear membrane
	10. cell wall, vacuole, chloroplast

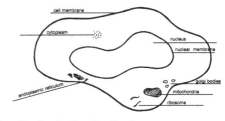

Animal Building Blocks page 163

1. cytoplasm	5. ribosome
2. endoplasmic reticulum	6. nuclear membrane
3. golgi bodies	7. nucleus
4. mitochondria	8. cell membrane

Now You See It, Now You Don't page 164

1. so that they blend into the environment
2. from various species of animals

Places, Please page 165

1.	TERRAPIN	12.	MUSSEL
2.	GECKO	13.	CONCH
3.	STINKPOT	14.	ABALONE
4.	WHIPTAIL	15.	LIMPET
5.	SKINK	16.	TEGULA
6.	LIZARD	17.	SNAIL
7.	ANOLE	18.	PERIWINKLE
8.	BOWFIN	19.	SCALLOP
9.	COBIA		
10.	SNOOK		
11.	PERCH		

20. Into what two categories could your "left-over" animals be placed?
birds and insects

Label Liabilities page 166

1. B	6. C	11. C
2. C	7. A	12. B
3. A	8. B	13. A
4. C	9. B	14. C
5. B	10. A	

Pictures in the Sky page 167

1. Big Dipper or Ursa Major
2. Little Dipper or Ursa Minor
3. Orion
4. Cygnus—the swan
5. Eagle—Aquilla
6. Auriga
7. Canus Major or the Big Dog

IF8679 A Little Bit of Everything

Royal Family in the Heavens
page 168
A. Cephus
B. Pegasus
C. Cassiopeia
D. Andromeda
E. Perseus

The Zodiac
page 169
1. Sagittarius
2. Aquarius
3. Aries
4. Gemini
5. Leo
6. Libra
7. Capricorn
8. Pisces
9. Taurus
10. Cancer
11. Virgo
12. Scorpio

Planetary Numbers
page 170

A. 3	B. 4	C. 3
1	3	5
6	9	2
9	2	4
7	6	8
4	1	1
8	7	6
5	8	7
2	5	9

D. Mars—687 days
Earth—365 days
Pluto—248 years
Venus—225 days
Saturn—29½ years
Mercury—88 days
Uranus—84 years
Neptune—165 years
Jupiter—12 years

E. Number of moons

Solar Calculations
page 171
1. 93,000,000 miles
2. A. 1,690,909 hours
B. 70,455 days
C. 193 years
D. 101,454,540 minutes
E. 6,087,272,400 seconds
3. six billion, eighty-seven million, two hundred seventy-two thousand, four hundred
4. A. 163,680,000,000 yards
B. 491,040,000,000
C. 149,800,000
D. 149,800,000,000 kilometers
5. It would take the same amount of time. Distances are all the same; only the units are different.

Space-Age Phenomena
page 172
1. black hole
2. supernova
3. rainbow
4. red giant
5. sunspots
6. neutron star
7. solar eclipse
8. asteroid belt
9. northern lights
10. white dwarf
11. Saturn's rings
12. shooting star
13. thunderstorm
14. meteor shower
15. solar flares

In Your Own Words
page 173
Answers will vary.

Ant Study
page 174
Students may choose any kind of ant to study. Physical characteristics and behaviors will depend on the type of ant chosen. The more interesting types are

Army ants
Fire ants
Bulldog ants
Leaf-cutter ants

Amazon Ants
Ponerine Ants
Carpenter Ants

The queen is mother and founder of the colony. She spends her entire life laying eggs. New queens come from female eggs that have been fertilized by the queen from her sperm sac. Most ants live only 6-10 weeks but certain queens live 15 years.

Nursemaids, food gatherers, and the queen's attendants are workers. Sterile females, or workers, do all the work necessary to keep the colony in good working order. They care for the young, enlarge the nest, and gather food for the queen and all the other ants in the colony. Larger ants or soldiers (guards) defend the nest. They also raid other nests and sometimes capture slaves.

An ant's life cycle has four stages: egg, larva, pupa, and adult.

Spider Web Observations
page 175
Answers will vary.

Symbol Sense
page 176
A. 6
B. 10
C. 1
D. 16
E. 14
F. 2
G. 13
H. 4
I. 9
J. extra description
K. 11
L. 8
M. 3
N. extra description

Search High and Low
page 178
1. T
2. F, Honolulu
3. M
4. F, Fairbanks
5. T
6. T
7. M
8. T
9. F
10. F, 46
11. M
12. T
13. M
14. F
15. T

Weather Trivia
page 179
1. A. troposphere
   B. stratosphere
   C. ionosphere
   D. exosphere
2. 23½
3. March 21 and Sept 23
4. equal nights
5. an instrument that measures the speed of wind
6. atmospheric pressure
7. humidity
8. USA, over 500
9. low
10. hurricanes
11. typhoons or cyclones
12. cirrus, cumulus, stratus
13. rain
14. clockwise
15. areas around the equator
16. mid-latitude mountainous regions (such as the Rocky Mountains in the United States)

Comparing Climates
page 180
Answers will vary.

Digging for Bones
page 181

Bone Strength
page 182
Round bones like those in the arms and legs provide better support than flat bones. Because they are stronger, they resist injury better than flat bones. Flat bones, like the ribs, provide better protection.

The Shrink Test
page 183
Answers will vary.

Sickly Sleuthwork page 187

1. S
2. E
3. E
4. Y
5. O
6. U
7. R
8. D
9. O
10. C
11. T
12. O
13. R
14. S
15. O
16. O
17. N

Before page 189
Answers will vary.

Preposterous Publicity page 191
A. kindergarten, 1832   B. skateboard, 1966

Keyboard Quest page 192
Answers will vary greatly. Here are some possible outcomes.
- A. 4-letter words: crew, ever, free, race, wage
  5-letter words: brace, grass, start, waste, zebra
  6+-letter words: career, regret   Longest: ???
- B. 4-letter: jump, kiln, moon, only, pink, pony
  5-letter: holly, knoll, milky, plump, nippy
  6+-letter: monopoly, lollipop   Longest: ???
- C. 4-letter: adds, dash, gala, glad, hash
  5-letter: flash, flask, glass, salad, shall
  6+-letter: salads, flasks
- D. 4-letter: coal, down, fork, kept, lend, name
  5-letter: blame, gland, panel, right, quake, shame
  6+-letter: height, turkey, toxicity   Longest: ???

Chip, Chip Hooray! page 193
1. 7
2. 2
3. 5
4. 3
5. 9
6. 1
7. 8
8. 10
9. 6
10. 4

Newton's Laws page 194
1. 3
2. 1
3. 2
4. 2
5. 1
6. 3
7. 1
8. 2
9. 3
10. 3

Drawing Atoms page 195

Blown Away page 200
Hurricane—a powerful rainstorm with driving winds. Occur near coastal areas. Secure your property—board up windows. Listen to weather service report. Evacuate if they tell you to. Otherwise stay in sheltered area away from windows.
Tornado—a powerful twisting windstorm. Go to a storm cellar or basement. If not available, go to a hallway or bathtub (away from windows). If outside, go to a ditch and lie down.
Blizzard—a snowstorm with winds of 35 mph or greater. Visibility is less than 500 feet. Stay indoors. If outside, keep mouth and nose covered and keep moving so you do not freeze. Try to follow a road or fence to a safe place.
Earthquake—heavy ground tremors. Stay inside. Go under a heavy desk or in an empty corner where falling objects will not hit you. If outdoors, stay away from buildings, trees, and power lines.
Electrical storm—lightning, thunderstorm. Stay away from water and electric power lines if outside. Inside—unplug electrical appliances.

What Would You Do? page 201
1. Since he is able to breathe, wait and see if he will cough up the obstruction. If he stops breathing, administer the abdominal thrust.
2. Send someone for help. Move him to a cool, shady place. Give him water.
3. Wrap with clean cloth, apply pressure. If there is no fracture, elevate wound above heart. Go for help.
4. Immobilize it with a splint. Go for help.
5. Call 911. Put the arm in cool water. Keep her calm until help arrives.
6. Do not rub her fingertips. If ski patrol is available, ask for help. If not, ski immediately to the closest shelter. Soak in tepid water once inside.
7. Call 911 and follow their instructions. Do not move him.
8. Send someone for help. Clear away anything the victim might hurt himself on.
9. Have someone get the troop leader. Give him a piece of candy, or any food or drink available (except diet drinks).
10. Call 911. It might be heart attack symptoms. He should get to a doctor.

Music and Math Connections page 202

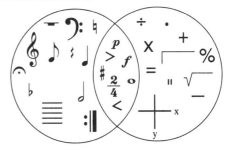

Musical Words page 203
Staff 1: egg, bed, cab, bead
Staff 2: fad, dad, feed, deaf

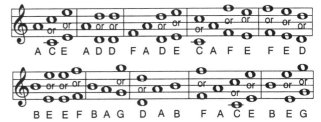

Great Composers page 205
1. Wolfgang Amadeus Mozart—**Eine kleine Nachtmusik**
2. Johann S. Bach—the **Brandenburg Concertos**
3. Ludwig van Beethoven—"Ode to Joy"
4. Johannes Brahms—"Lullaby"
5. Joseph Haydn—"Farewell Symphony"
6. Peter I. Tchaikovsky—"Nutcracker Suite"

Color Wheel page 207

Mystery Picture

page 209

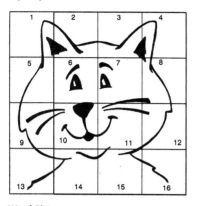

Word Pictures

page 214

1. turn over a new leaf
2. through thick and thin
3. needle in a haystack
4. full of oneself
5. all in all
6. add insult to injury
7. few and far between
8. hit below the belt
9. wolf in sheep's clothing
10. hang around
11. fish out of water
12. bend over backward
13. draw a blank
14. once upon a time

Word Pictures II

page 215

1. read between the lines
2. half the battle is won
3. rest in peace
4. safety in numbers
5. hole in one
6. don't put all your eggs in one basket
7. go up in smoke
8. skating on thin ice
9. you're on the ball
10. noel (no "L")
11. a bird in the hand is worth two in the bush
12. don't give up
13. find out the hard way
14. misunderstanding between friends

I.Q. Test

page 216

All that should be on the test is the student's name.

Which One?

page 218

1. They are the same.
2. They are the same
3. They are the same.
4. They are the same.
5. the middle line
6. They are the same.
7. either
8. same
9. either
10. either

Is It Possible?

page 219

1. yes
2. both
3. yes
4. no
5. no
6. two the's
7. both
8. They are all top and all bottom
9. hold the paper close to your eyes
10. yes

Seeing Is Believing

page 220

1.

2. green circle and purple square
3. green circle and orange square
4. the complement of the color used

Mission Possible

page 221

Fold corner up. Draw dot and most of circle. Fold corner back and finish circle.

How Well Do You Remember?

page 222

1. 3:00
2. 3 cars, 1 truck
3. Elm
4. winter
5. 10
6. cat, 2 dogs, rabbit, bird
7. no
8. 819
9. east
10. yes
11. stop sign
12. yes
13. Oak
14. $3.00
15. man

Brain Teasers

page 224

1. March
2. amendment
3. Japan
4. past
5. pot
6. sculling team
7. talkies
8. engineer
9. eerie
10. rickshaw

Wally's Wacky Word Processor

page 226

1. number of syllables or number of vowels
2. number of consonants
3. number of different vowels
4. number of different consonants
5. words and numbers that sound the same

English Sense

page 227

1. house, houses
2. boot, boots
3. box, boxes
4. apply, applied
5. read, read
6. free, freed